WHAT'S COOKING
baking

Emma Patmore

THUNDER BAY
P·R·E·S·S

Published by
Thunder Bay Press
5880 Oberlin Drive, Suite 400
San Diego, California 92121
1–800–284–3580

http:/www.advmkt.com

Library of Congress Cataloging in Publication Data

Patmore, Emma.
  What's Cooking Baking / Emma Patmore.
    p. cm.
  Includes index.
  ISBN 1–57145–148–X
  1. Cookery, Baking   I. Title
TX763.P28   1998   98-15354
641.8'15--dc21   CIP

Printed in China

3 4 5 99 00 01 02

Produced by Haldane Mason, London

Acknowledgments
Art Director: Ron Samuels
Editorial Director: Sydney Francis
Editorial Consultant: Christopher Fagg
Managing Editor: Jo-Anne Cox
Editor: Felicity Jackson
Design: Digital Artworks Partnership Ltd
Photography: Iain Bagwell
Home Economist: Emma Patmore

Note
Unless otherwise stated, milk is assumed to be full fat, eggs are medium,
and pepper is freshly ground black pepper.

Contents

Introduction

This beautifully illustrated book brings you all the skills you need to re-create some of the best-loved traditional baking dishes. It also shows you how to experiment with some of the exciting new ingredients now readily available in most supermarkets.

Clear step-by-step instructions guide you through the techniques needed to master all those baking favorites that have been savored and enjoyed from generation to generation.

PUDDINGS & PASTRIES

Experience the sweet pleasure of a wonderful selection of everyday and special occasion desserts in Chapter 1 as it shows you how to make rich, sticky, and irresistible desserts, such as Pavlova, Fruit Crumble, Queen of Puddings, and tasty sticky chocolate puddings. Everyone's favorite is sure to be included.

This chapter also helps you to perfect your pastry so that you are guaranteed success with such timeless classics as Syrup Tart, Apricot & Cranberry Frangipane, Apple Tart Tatin, Custard Tart, and Cheese & Apple Tart.

BREADS & SIDE DISHES

Making bread at home is great fun and allows you to experiment with all sorts of ingredients, such as sun-dried tomatoes, garlic, mangoes, and olive oil, to create versatile and delicious variations of modern breads, rolls, and loaves. Chapter 2 also shows you how to spice up all sorts of side dishes with exciting adaptations of traditional flans, pies, and scones, such as Cheese & Mustard Scones, tasty Cheese Pudding, Onion Tart, and delicious Celery & Onion Pies.

VEGETARIAN COOKING

Vegetarian recipes full of delicious wholesome ingredients, which are every bit as good as traditional baking favorites, have been created in Chapter 3. Recipes include Lentil & Red Bell Pepper Flan, Date & Apricot Tart, Pineapple Upside-down Cake, and Brazil Nut & Mushroom Pie.

CAKES & COOKIES

Transform traditional cakes and cookies into a real extravaganza with some new adaptations of old favorites in Chapters 4 and 5.

Irresistible cake recipes, such as Marbled Chocolate Cake, Olive Oil Fruit & Nut Cake, Gingerbread, and Meringues, are included as are delicious cookie recipes, such as Chocolate Chip Cookies and Gingernuts. These recipes are quick and easy to make and are guaranteed to be winners with the whole family.

MAKING CAKES

With all baking recipes, there are some basic principles that apply and this is especially true of cake making:

- Start by reading the recipe all the way through.

- Measure all the ingredients accurately and do basic preparation, such as grating and chopping, before you start cooking.

- Basic cake-making ingredients should kept be at room temperature.

- Mixtures that are creamed together, a process which involves beating butter and sugar together, should be almost white and have a "soft dropping" consistency. This can be done by hand, but an electric mixer will save you time and effort.

- "Folding in" is achieved by using a metal spoon or spatula and working as gently as possible to fold through the flour or dry ingredients in a figure-eight movement.

- Do not remove a cake from the oven until it is fully cooked. To test if a cake is cooked, press the surface lightly with your fingertips—it should feel springy to the touch. Alternatively, insert a toothpick into the center of the cake—it will come out clean if the cake is cooked through.

- Leave cakes in their pans to cool before carefully turning out onto a wire rack to cool completely.

MAKING PIES & TARTS

When making the pies or tarts in the book, follow these basic principles:

- Sift the dry ingredients into a large mixing bowl, add the diced butter, and toss it through the flour.

- Gently rub the butter between your fingertips, a little at a time, until the mixture looks like fine breadcrumbs and, as you rub in the mixture, lift your hands up to aerate the mixture as it falls back into the bowl.

- Bind the mixture with iced water or other liquid, using just enough to make a soft dough. Wrap the dough and chill for at least 30 minutes.

Puddings & Pastries

No meal is really complete without a dessert, and this chapter indulges the reader with a hearty and wholesome collection of some best-loved recipes. Fruit puddings, chocolate puddings, lemon puddings, and crumbly puddings—they are all fun, easy to make, and delicious. This chapter also offers some new surprises for old-fashioned puddings, leaving you with the difficult decision of which to try first; will it be Plum Cobbler or Mini Frangipane Tarts with Lime?

Soft, crumbly, and melt-in-your-mouth pastry holds the secret to success with a wide variety of magnificent dishes. Pie dough is used in several recipes in this chapter, and it is important to remember that a light touch when preparing the dough will give a much better result.

Where "fresh ready-made pie dough" and "fresh ready-made puff pastry" is specified in the recipes, the quality that you get from the supermarket products is extremely good and saves you time on certain recipes.

Eve's Pudding

*This is pudding has soft apples
on the bottom and a light buttery sponge on top.*

Serves 6

INGREDIENTS

1 pound cooking apples, peeled,
   cored, and sliced
1/3 cup granulated sugar
1 tbsp lemon juice
1/3 cup golden raisins

1/3 cup butter
1/3 cup superfine sugar
1 egg, beaten
1 1/4 cups self-rising flour
3 tbsp milk

1/4 cup slivered almonds
custard or heavy cream,
   to serve

1 Thoroughly grease a 3½ cup ovenproof dish.

2 Mix the apples with the sugar, lemon juice, and golden raisins. Spoon the mixture into the greased dish.

3 In a bowl, cream the butter and superfine sugar together until pale. Add the egg, a little at a time.

4 Carefully fold in the self-rising flour and stir in the milk to give a soft, dropping consistency.

5 Spread the mixture over the apples and sprinkle with the slivered almonds.

6 Bake in a preheated oven at 350°F for 40–45 minutes, until the sponge is a light golden brown color.

7 Serve the pudding piping hot, accompanied by custard or heavy cream.

COOK'S TIP

To increase the almond flavor of this apple pudding, add 1/4 cup ground almonds with the flour in step 4.

Queen of Puddings

A slightly different version of this old favorite, made with the addition of orange rind and marmalade to give a delicious orange flavor.

Serves 8

INGREDIENTS

2 $^1/_2$ cups milk

2 tbsp butter

1 $^1/_4$ cups superfine sugar

finely grated rind of 1 orange

4 eggs, separated

$^3/_4$ cup fresh breadcrumbs

pinch of salt

6 tbsp orange marmalade

1 Thoroughly grease a 6 cup ovenproof dish.

2 To make the custard, heat the milk in a pan with the butter, $^1/_4$ cup of the superfine sugar, and the grated orange rind until just warm.

3 Whisk the egg yolks in a bowl. Gradually pour the warm milk over the eggs, stirring.

4 Stir the breadcrumbs into the pan, then transfer the mixture to the prepared dish, and let stand for 15 minutes.

5 Bake in a preheated oven at 350°F for 20–25 minutes, until the custard has just set. Remove the custard from the oven, but do not turn the oven off.

6 To make the meringue, whisk the egg whites with a pinch of salt until they stand in soft peaks. Whisk in the remaining sugar, a little at a time.

7 Spread the orange marmalade over the cooked custard. Top with the meringue, spreading it right to the edges of the dish.

8 Return the pudding to the oven and bake for a further 20 minutes, until the meringue is crisp and golden.

COOK'S TIP

If you prefer a crisper meringue, bake the pudding in the oven for an extra 5 minutes.

Bread & Butter Pudding

A traditional pudding full of fruit and spices.
It is the perfect way to use up day-old bread.

Serves 6

INGREDIENTS

7 ounces white bread, sliced
4 tbsp butter, softened
2 tbsp golden raisins

$\frac{1}{8}$ cup candied peel
2 $\frac{1}{2}$ cups milk
4 egg yolks

$\frac{1}{3}$ cup superfine sugar
$\frac{1}{2}$ tsp apple pie spice

1 Thoroughly grease a 5$\frac{1}{3}$ cup ovenproof dish.

2 Remove the crusts from the bread (optional), spread with the butter, and cut the slices in half.

3 Arrange half of the buttered bread slices in the prepared ovenproof dish. Sprinkle half of the golden raisins and candied peel over the top of the bread.

4 Place the remaining bread slices over the fruit, and then top with the reserved fruit.

5 To make the custard, bring the milk almost to a boil in a saucepan. Whisk together the egg yolks and the sugar in a bowl, then pour in the warm milk.

6 Pour the warm custard through a strainer. Then pour the custard over the bread slices.

7 Let stand for 30 minutes, then sprinkle with the apple pie spice.

8 Place the ovenproof dish in a roasting pan half-filled with hot water.

9 Bake in a preheated oven at 400°F for 40–45 minutes, until the pudding has just set. Serve warm.

COOK'S TIP

The pudding can be prepared in advance up to step 7, and then set aside until required.

Plum Cobbler

This dessert can be adapted to suit
all types of fruit if plums are not available.

Serves 6

INGREDIENTS

$2\frac{1}{4}$ pounds plums, pits removed, and
 sliced
$\frac{1}{3}$ cup superfine sugar
1 tbsp lemon juice

$2\frac{1}{4}$ cups all-purpose flour
$\frac{1}{3}$ cup granulated sugar
2 tsp baking powder
1 egg, beaten

$\frac{2}{3}$ cup buttermilk
6 tbsp butter, melted and cooled
heavy cream, to serve

1 Lightly grease an 8 cup ovenproof dish.

2 In a large bowl, mix together the plums, superfine sugar, lemon juice, and $\frac{1}{4}$ cup of the all-purpose flour.

3 Spoon the coated plums into the bottom of the prepared ovenproof dish.

4 Mix together the remaining flour, granulated sugar, and baking powder in a bowl until well combined.

5 Add the beaten egg, buttermilk, and cooled melted butter. Mix everything gently together to form a soft dough.

6 Place spoonfuls of the dough on top of the fruit mixture until it is almost covered.

7 Bake the cobbler in a preheated oven at 375°F for about 35–40 minutes, until golden brown and bubbling.

8 Serve the pudding piping hot, with heavy cream.

COOK'S TIP

If you cannot find buttermilk, try using sour cream.

Blackberry Pudding

A delicious dessert to make when blackberries are in abundance!
If blackberries are unavailable, use other fruits, such as currants or gooseberries.

Serves 4

INGREDIENTS

1 pound blackberries
1/3 cup superfine sugar
1 egg

1/3 cup light brown sugar
6 tbsp butter, melted

8 tbsp milk
1 cup self-rising flour

1 Lightly grease a large 3½ cup ovenproof dish.

2 In a large mixing bowl, gently mix together the blackberries and superfine sugar until they are thoroughly combined.

3 Transfer the blackberry and sugar mixture to the prepared ovenproof dish.

4 Beat together the egg and light brown sugar in a separate mixing bowl until well combined. Stir in the melted butter and milk.

5 Sift the flour into the egg and butter mixture and fold together lightly to form a smooth batter.

6 Carefully spread the batter over the blackberry and sugar mixture in the ovenproof dish.

7 Bake the pudding in a preheated oven at 350°F for about 25–30 minutes, until the topping is firm and golden.

8 Sprinkle the pudding with a little sugar, if desired, and serve hot.

VARIATION

You can add 2 tablespoons of unsweetened cocoa to the batter in step 5, if you prefer a chocolate flavor.

Raspberry Shortcake

For this lovely summery dessert, two crisp rounds of shortbread are sandwiched together with fresh raspberries and whipped cream.

Serves 8

INGREDIENTS

$1^1/_2$ cups self-rising flour
7 tbsp butter, cut into cubes
$^1/_3$ cup superfine sugar
1 egg yolk
1 tbsp rose water

$2^1/_2$ cups whipping cream,
  whipped lightly
$1^1/_3$ cups raspberries, plus a few
  for decoration

TO DECORATE:
confectioners' sugar
mint leaves

1 Lightly grease 2 cookie sheets.

2 To make the shortcakes, sift the flour into a bowl.

3 Rub the butter into the flour with your fingers until the mixture resembles breadcrumbs.

4 Stir the sugar, egg yolk, and rose water into the mixture and bring together with your fingertips to form a soft dough. Divide the dough in half.

5 Roll each piece of dough to an 8-inch round and place each one onto a prepared cookie sheet. Crimp the edges of the dough.

6 Bake in a preheated oven at 375°F for 15 minutes, until lightly golden. Transfer the shortcakes to a wire rack and let cool.

7 Mix the cream with the raspberries and spoon on top of one of the shortcake rounds. Top with the other shortcake

round, dust with a little confectioners' sugar, and decorate with the extra raspberries and mint leaves.

COOK'S TIP

The shortcake can be made a few days in advance and stored in an airtight container until required.

3

4

5

Pavlova

This delicious dessert originated in Australia. Serve it with sharp fruits to balance the sweetness of the meringue.

Serves 6

INGREDIENTS

3 egg whites
pinch of salt
³/₄ cup superfine sugar

1¹/₄ cups heavy cream, lightly whipped

fresh fruit of your choice (raspberries, strawberries, peaches, passion fruit, ground cherries)

1 Line a large cookie sheet with a sheet of baking parchment.

2 Whisk the egg whites with the salt in a large bowl until they form soft peaks.

3 Whisk in the sugar a little at a time, whisking well after each addition until all of the sugar has been incorporated.

4 Spoon three-quarters of the meringue onto the cookie sheet, forming a round 8 inches in diameter.

5 Place spoonfuls of the remaining meringue all around the edge of the round so they join up to make a nest shape.

6 Bake in a preheated oven at 275°F for 1¹/₄ hours.

7 Turn the heat off, but leave the pavlova in the oven until it is completely cold.

8 To serve, transfer the pavlova to a serving dish. Gently spread with the lightly whipped heavy cream, then arrange the fresh fruit on top.

COOK'S TIP

It is a good idea to make the pavlova in the evening and leave it in the turned-off oven overnight.

COOK'S TIP

If you have difficulty making the round shape, draw a circle on the baking parchment, turn the paper over, then spoon the meringue inside the shape.

Sticky Chocolate Pudding

These individual puddings always look impressive at the end of a meal.

Serves 6

INGREDIENTS

¹/2 cup butter, softened
³/4 cup light brown sugar
3 eggs, beaten
pinch of salt
¹/4 cup unsweetened cocoa
1 cup self-rising flour

1 ounce dark chocolate,
   finely chopped
2³/4 ounces white chocolate,
   finely chopped

SAUCE:
²/3 cup heavy cream
¹/3 cup light brown sugar
2 tbsp butter

1 Lightly grease 6 individual ³/4 cup pudding molds with a little butter.

2 In a bowl, cream together the butter and sugar until pale and fluffy. Beat in the eggs, a little at a time, beating well after each addition.

3 Sift the salt, unsweetened cocoa, and flour into the creamed mixture and fold through the mixture. Stir the chopped chocolate into the mixture until evenly combined.

4 Divide the mixture between the prepared pudding molds. Lightly grease 6 squares of foil and use them to cover the tops of the molds. Press around the edges to seal.

5 Place the molds in a roasting pan and pour in boiling water to come halfway up the sides of the molds.

6 Bake in a preheated oven at 350°F for 50 minutes, or until a toothpick inserted into the center comes out clean.

7 Remove the molds from the roasting pan and set aside while you prepare the sauce.

8 To make the sauce, put the cream, sugar, and butter into a pan and bring to a boil over a gentle heat. Simmer gently until the sugar has dissolved.

9 To serve, run a knife around the edge of each pudding, then turn out onto individual serving plates. Pour the sauce over the top of the puddings and serve immediately.

Chocolate Brownie Roulade

The addition of nuts and raisins has given this dessert extra texture,
making it similar to that of chocolate brownies.

Serves 8

INGREDIENTS

$5^{1}/_{2}$ ounces dark chocolate, broken into pieces
3 tbsp water
$^{3}/_{4}$ cup superfine sugar
5 eggs, separated

2 tbsp raisins, chopped
$^{1}/_{4}$ cup chopped pecans
pinch of salt

$1^{1}/_{4}$ cups heavy cream, whipped lightly
confectioners' sugar, for dusting

1 Grease a 12 x 8-inch jelly roll pan, line with baking parchment, and thoroughly grease the parchment.

2 Heat the chocolate with the water in a small saucepan over a low heat until the chocolate has just melted. Let cool.

3 In a bowl, whisk the sugar and egg yolks for 2–3 minutes with a hand-held electric mixer until thick and pale.

4 Fold in the cooled chocolate, raisins, and pecans.

5 In a separate bowl, whisk the egg whites with the salt. Fold one-quarter of the egg whites into the chocolate mixture, then fold in the rest of the whites, working lightly and quickly.

6 Transfer the mixture to the prepared pan and bake in a preheated oven at 350°F for 25 minutes, until risen and just firm to the touch. Remove from the oven and let cool before covering with a sheet of nonstick baking parchment and a damp clean dish cloth. Leave until completely cold.

7 Turn the roulade out onto another piece of baking parchment dusted with confectioners' sugar and remove the lining paper.

8 Spread the whipped heavy cream over the roulade. Starting from a short end, roll the sponge away from you using the paper to guide you. Trim the ends of the roulade to make a neat finish and transfer to a serving plate. Chill in the refrigerator until ready to serve. Dust with a little confectioners' sugar before serving, if desired.

One Roll Fruit Pie

This is an easy way to make a pie, once you have rolled out the pie dough and filled it with fruit, you just turn the edges of the pie dough in! The pie is excellent served with ice cream.

Serves 8

INGREDIENTS

PIE DOUGH:
1¹/₂ cups all-purpose flour
7 tbsp butter, cut into
   small pieces
1 tbsp water
1 egg, separated

sugar cubes, crushed, for sprinkling

FILLING:
1¹/₂ pound prepared fruit (rhubarb,
   gooseberries, plums, damsons)

6 tbsp light brown sugar
1 tbsp ground ginger

1 Thoroughly grease a large cookie sheet with a little butter.

2 To make the pie dough, place the flour and butter in a mixing bowl and rub in the butter with your fingers. Add the water and work the mixture together until a soft pie dough has formed. Wrap and chill for 30 minutes.

3 Roll out the chilled pie dough to a round measuring about 14 inches in diameter.

4 Transfer the round to the center of the greased cookie sheet. Brush the pie dough with the egg yolk.

5 To make the filling, mix the prepared fruit with the brown sugar and ground ginger and pile it into the center of the pie dough.

6 Turn in the edges of the pie dough all the way around. Brush the surface of the pie dough with the egg white and

sprinkle evenly with the crushed sugar cubes.

7 Bake in a preheated oven at 400°F for 35 minutes, or until golden brown. Serve warm.

COOK'S TIP

If the pie dough breaks when shaping it into a round, just patch and seal, as the overall effect of this tart is rough.

Fruit Crumble Tart

This tart has a double helping of flavors, with the fruit filling covered in a crumbly topping.

Serves 8

INGREDIENTS

PIE DOUGH:
1 1/4 cups all-purpose flour
5 tsp superfine sugar
9 tbsp butter, cut into small pieces
1 tbsp water

FILLING:
1 1/2 cups raspberries
1 pound plums, halved, pitted, and roughly chopped
3 tbsp raw crystal sugar

TO SERVE:
light cream

TOPPING:
1 cup all-purpose flour
1/3 cup raw crystal sugar
1/3 cup butter, cut into small pieces
1 cup chopped mixed nuts
1 tsp ground cinnamon

1 To make the pie dough, place the flour, sugar, and butter in a bowl and rub in the butter with your fingers. Add the water and work the mixture together until a soft pie dough has formed. Wrap and chill for 30 minutes.

2 Roll out the pie dough to line the base of a 10-inch loose-bottomed quiche pan. Prick the base of the pie dough with a fork and chill for about 30 minutes.

3 To make the filling, toss the raspberries and plums together with the sugar and spoon into the pie shell.

4 To make the crumble topping, combine the flour, sugar, and butter in a bowl. Work the butter into the flour with your fingers until the mixture resembles coarse breadcrumbs. Stir in the nuts and ground cinnamon.

5 Sprinkle the topping over the fruit and bake in a preheated oven at 400°F for 20–25 minutes, until the topping is golden. Serve with light cream.

Cheese & Apple Tart

The chopped apples and dates and the brown sugar in the filling make this a sweet tart with a savory twist to it!

Serves 8

INGREDIENTS

1¹/₂ cups self-rising flour
1 tsp baking powder
pinch of salt
¹/₃ cup light brown sugar

³/₄ cup pitted dates, chopped
1 pound 2 ounces eating apples,
    cored and chopped
¹/₂ cup chopped walnuts

¹/₄ cup sunflower oil
2 eggs
1¹/₂ cups grated Red Leicester cheese

1 Grease a 10-inch loose-bottomed quiche pan with a little butter and line with baking parchment.

2 Sift the flour, baking powder, and salt into a bowl. Stir in the brown sugar and the chopped dates, apples, and walnuts. Thoroughly mix together until well combined.

3 Beat the oil and eggs together and add the mixture to the dry ingredients. Stir until thoroughly combined.

4 Spoon half of the mixture into the pan and level the surface with the back of a spoon.

5 Sprinkle with the cheese, then spoon over the remaining cake mixture, spreading it to the edges of the pan.

6 Bake in a preheated oven at 350°F for 45–50 minutes, or until golden brown and firm to the touch.

7 Cool slightly in the pan. Serve warm.

COOK'S TIP

This is a deliciously moist tart. Any leftovers should be stored in the refrigerator and heated to serve.

Apple Tart Tatin

*This French upside-down tart is always a popular
choice for a comforting dessert.*

Serves 8

INGREDIENTS

9 tbsp butter
$1/_2$ cup superfine sugar

4 eating apples, cored and quartered
9 ounces fresh ready-made
pie dough

crème fraîche, to serve

1 Heat the butter and sugar in a
9-inch ovenproof skillet over
a medium heat for about
5 minutes, until the mixture
begins to caramelize. Remove the
skillet from the heat.

2 Arrange the apple quarters,
skin side down, in the skillet,
taking care as the butter and sugar
are very hot. Place the skillet back
on the heat and simmer for
2 minutes.

3 On a lightly floured surface,
roll out the pie dough to
form a round just a little larger
than the skillet.

4 Place the pie dough over the
apples, press down, and tuck
in the edges to seal the apples
under the layer of pie dough.

5 Bake in a preheated oven at
400°F for 20–25 minutes,
until the pie dough is golden.
Remove from the oven and let
cool for about 10 minutes.

6 Place a serving plate over the
skillet and invert so that the
pastry forms the base of the
turned-out tart. Serve warm with
crème fraîche.

VARIATION

*Replace the apples with
pears, if you prefer. Leave
the skin on the pears, cut
them into quarters, and then
remove the cores.*

Syrup Tart

This is an old-fashioned pudding which still delights people time after time. It is very quick to make if you use ready-made pastry.

Serves 8

INGREDIENTS

9 ounces fresh ready-made
pie dough
1 cup light corn syrup

2 cups fresh white breadcrumbs
$1/2$ cup heavy cream

finely grated rind of $1/2$ lemon
or orange
2 tbsp lemon or orange juice
custard, to serve

1 Roll out the pie dough to line an 8-inch loose-bottomed quiche pan, reserving the pie dough trimmings. Prick the base of the pie dough with a fork and chill in the refrigerator.

2 Cut out small shapes from the reserved pie dough trimmings, such as leaves, stars, or hearts, to decorate the top of the syrup tart.

3 In a bowl, mix together the corn syrup, breadcrumbs, cream, grated lemon or orange rind, and lemon or orange juice.

4 Pour the mixture into the pie shell and decorate the edges of the tart with the pie dough cut-outs.

5 Bake in a preheated oven at 375°F for 35–40 minutes, or until the filling is just set.

6 Leave the tart to cool slightly in the pan. Turn out and serve with custard.

VARIATION

Use the pie dough trimmings to create a lattice pattern on top of the tart, if preferred.

Apple & Mincemeat Tart

*The fresh apple brings out the flavor of the sweet rich mincemeat
and makes it a beautifully moist filling for pies and tarts.*

Serves 8

INGREDIENTS

PIE DOUGH:
1¼ cups all-purpose flour
2 tbsp superfine sugar

½ cup butter, cut into
 small pieces
1 tbsp water

FILLING:
14½ ounce jar mincemeat
3 eating apples, cored and grated
1 tbsp lemon juice
6 tsp light corn syrup
3 tbsp butter

1 To make the pie dough, place the flour and superfine sugar in a large mixing bowl, add the butter, and rub in with your fingertips.

2 Add the water and work the mixture together until a soft pie dough has formed. Wrap and chill in the refrigerator for 30 minutes.

3 On a lightly floured surface, roll out the dough and line a 10-inch loose-bottomed quiche pan. Prick the dough with a fork and chill in the refrigerator for 30 minutes.

4 Line the pie shell with foil and dried beans. Bake the shell in a preheated oven at 375°F for 15 minutes. Remove the foil and beans and cook the shell for a further 15 minutes.

5 Mix the mincemeat with the apples and lemon juice until well combined and spoon into the baked pie shell.

6 Melt the syrup and butter together and pour over the mincemeat mixture.

7 Return the tart to the oven and bake for about 20 minutes, until firm. Serve warm.

VARIATION

Add 2 tbsp sherry to spice up the mincemeat, if you wish.

Custard Tart

*This is a classic egg custard tart which should be served
as fresh as possible for the best flavor and texture.*

Serves 8

INGREDIENTS

PIE DOUGH;
1¼ cups all-purpose flour
5 tsp superfine sugar
½ cup butter, cut into small pieces
1 tbsp water

FILLING:
3 eggs
⅔ cup light cream
⅔ cup milk
freshly grated nutmeg

TO SERVE:
whipped cream

1 To make the pie dough, place the flour and sugar in a mixing bowl and rub in the butter with your fingertips.

2 Add the water and mix together until a soft pie dough has formed. Wrap and chill in the refrigerator for about 30 minutes.

3 Roll out the dough to form a round slightly larger than a 10-inch loose-bottomed quiche pan.

4 Line the pan with the dough, trimming off the edges. Prick the dough with a fork and chill in the refrigerator for 30 minutes.

5 Line the pie shell with a sheet of foil and dried beans.

6 Bake in a preheated oven at 375°F for 15 minutes. Remove the foil and beans and bake the pie shell for a further 15 minutes.

7 To make the filling, whisk together the eggs, cream, milk, and nutmeg. Pour the filling into the prepared pie shell. Transfer the tart to the oven and cook for 25–30 minutes, or until just set. Serve with whipped cream, if desired.

COOK'S TIP

Baking the pie shell first ensures that the finished tart has a really crisp base.

Lemon Tart

*No one will be able to resist this tart with its buttery pastry
and a sharp, melt-in-your-mouth lemon filling.*

Serves 8

INGREDIENTS

PIE DOUGH:
1 1/4 cups all-purpose flour
5 tsp superfine sugar
1/2 cup butter, cut into small pieces
1 tbsp water

FILLING:
2/3 cup heavy cream
1/2 cup superfine sugar
4 eggs
grated rind of 3 lemons
12 tbsp lemon juice
confectioners' sugar, for dusting

1 To make the pie dough, place the flour and sugar in a bowl and rub in the butter using your fingertips. Add the water and mix until a soft pie dough has formed. Wrap and chill for 30 minutes.

2 On a lightly floured surface, roll out the dough and line a 10-inch loose-bottomed quiche pan. Prick the pie dough all over with a fork and chill for 30 minutes.

3 Line the pie shell with foil and dried beans and bake in a preheated oven at 375°F for 15 minutes. Remove the foil and beans, return to the oven and cook the pie shell for a further 15 minutes.

4 To make the filling, whisk the cream, sugar, eggs, and lemon rind and juice together. Place the pie shell, still in its pan, on a cookie sheet and pour in the filling.

5 Bake in the oven for about 20 minutes, or until just set. Let to cool, then lightly dust with confectioners' sugar before serving.

COOK'S TIP

To avoid any spillage, pour half of the filling into the pie shell, place in the oven, and pour in the remaining filling.

Orange Tart

*This is a variation of the classic lemon tart—in this recipe
fresh breadcrumbs are used to create a thicker texture.*

Serves 6–8

INGREDIENTS

PIE DOUGH:
1¼ cups all-purpose flour
5 tsp superfine sugar
½ cup butter, cut into
   small pieces
1 tbsp water

FILLING:
grated rind of 2 oranges
9 tbsp orange juice
⅞ cups fresh white breadcrumbs
2 tbsp lemon juice
⅔ cup light cream
¼ cup butter
¼ cup superfine sugar

2 eggs, separated
pinch of salt

1 To make the pie dough, place the flour and sugar in a large bowl and rub in the butter with your fingertips. Add the cold water and work the mixture together until a soft pie dough has formed. Wrap and chill for 30 minutes.

2 Roll out the dough and line a 10-inch loose-bottomed quiche pan. Prick the pie dough with a fork and chill for 30 minutes.

3 Line the pie shell with foil and dried beans and bake in a preheated oven at 375°F for 15 minutes. Remove the foil and beans and cook the pie shell for a further 15 minutes.

4 To make the filling, mix the orange rind and juice and the breadcrumbs in a bowl. Stir in the lemon juice and light cream. Melt the butter and sugar in a pan over a low heat. Remove the pan from the heat, add the 2 egg yolks, the

salt, and the breadcrumb mixture and stir to combine.

5 In a mixing bowl, whisk the egg whites with a pinch of salt until they form soft peaks. Carefully fold them into the egg yolk mixture.

6 Pour the filling mixture into the pie shell. Bake in a preheated oven at 325°F for about 45 minutes, or until just set. Cool slightly and serve warm.

Coconut Cream Tart

Decorate this tart with some fresh tropical fruit, such as mango or pineapple, and extra shredded coconut, toasted.

Serves 6–8

INGREDIENTS

PIE DOUGH:
1¼ cups all-purpose flour
5 tsp superfine sugar
½ cup butter, cut into
   small pieces
1 tbsp water

FILLING:
2 cups milk
4½ ounces creamed coconut
3 egg yolks
½ cup superfine sugar
½ cup all-purpose flour, sifted
⅓ cup shredded coconut
¼ cup chopped candied pineapple

2 tbsp rum or pineapple juice
1¼ cups whipping cream, whipped

1 To make the pie dough, place the flour and sugar in a bowl and rub in the butter with your fingertips. Add the water and work the mixture together until a soft pie dough has formed. Wrap and chill for 30 minutes.

2 On a lightly floured surface, roll out the dough and line a 10-inch loose-bottomed quiche pan. Prick the pie dough with a fork and chill for 30 minutes.

Line the pie shell with foil and dried beans and bake in a preheated oven at 375°F for 15 minutes. Remove the foil and beans and cook the pie shell for a further 15 minutes. Let cool.

3 To make the filling, bring the milk and creamed coconut to just below boiling point in a pan, stirring to melt the coconut.

4 In a bowl, whisk the egg yolks with the sugar until pale and fluffy. Whisk in the flour. Pour the hot milk over the egg mixture, stirring. Return the mixture to the pan and gently heat for 8 minutes, until thick, stirring. Let cool.

5 Stir in the candied pineapple, coconut, rum or pineapple juice, and spread the filling in the pie shell. Cover with the whipped cream and chill until required.

Pine Nut Tart

This tart has a sweet filling made with creamy cheese and it is topped
with pine nuts for a decorative finish.

Serves 8

INGREDIENTS

PIE DOUGH:
1¼ cups all-purpose flour
5 tsp superfine sugar
½ cup butter, cut into
  small pieces
1 tbsp water

FILLING:
1¼ cups cottage cheese
4 tbsp heavy cream
3 eggs
½ cup superfine sugar
grated rind of 1 orange
1 cup pine nuts

1 To make the pie dough, place the flour and sugar in a bowl and rub in the butter with your fingertips. Add the water and work the mixture together until a soft pie dough has formed. Wrap and chill for 30 minutes.

2 On a lightly floured surface, roll out the dough and line a 10-inch loose-bottomed quiche pan. Prick the pie dough all over with a fork and chill for 30 minutes.

3 Line the pie shell with foil and dried beans and bake in a preheated oven at 375°F for 15 minutes. Remove the foil and beans and cook the pie shell for a further 15 minutes.

4 To make the filling, beat together the curd cheese, cream, eggs, sugar, orange rind, and half of the pine nuts until well combined. Pour the filling into the preprared pie shell and sprinkle with the remaining pine nuts.

5 Bake in the oven at 325°F for 35 minutes, or until just set. Set aside and cool slightly before serving.

VARIATION

 You can replace the pine nuts with slivered almonds, if you prefer.

Candied Peel & Nut Tart

This very rich tart is not for the faint-hearted. Serve in thin slices.

Serves 8

INGREDIENTS

PIE DOUGH:
1¼ cups all-purpose flour
5 tsp superfine sugar
½ cup butter, cut into
   small pieces
1 tbsp water

FILLING:
6 tbsp butter
¼ cup superfine sugar
⅓ cup set honey
¾ cup heavy cream
1 egg, beaten

1¾ cups mixed nuts
⅞ cup candied peel

1 To make the pie dough, place the flour and sugar in a bowl and rub in the pieces of butter with your fingertips. Add the water and work the mixture together until a soft pie dough has formed. Wrap and chill for 30 minutes.

2 On a lightly floured surface, roll out the dough and line a 10-inch loose-bottomed quiche pan. Prick the pie dough all over with a fork and chill for 30 minutes.

3 Line the pie shell with foil and dried beans and bake in a preheated oven at 375°F for 15 minutes. Remove the foil and beans and cook for a further 15 minutes.

4 To make the filling, melt the butter, sugar, and honey in a small saucepan. Stir in the cream and beaten egg, then add the nuts and candied peel. Cook over a low heat for 2 minutes, until the mixture is a pale golden color, stirring constantly.

5 Pour the filling into the pie shell and bake for 15–20 minutes, or until just set. Let cool, then serve in slices.

VARIATION

Substitute walnuts or pecans for the mixed nuts, if you prefer.

Apricot & Cranberry Frangipane Tart

This tart is ideal to make at Christmastime when fresh cranberries are in abundance. If desired, brush the warm tart with 2 tablespoons of melted apricot preserve.

Serves 8–10

INGREDIENTS

PIE DOUGH:
1$1/4$ cups all-purpose flour
$1/2$ cup superfine sugar
$1/2$ cup butter, cut into
   small pieces
1 tbsp water

FILLING:
$7/8$ cup sweet butter
1 cup superfine sugar
1 egg
2 egg yolks
$1/3$ cup all-purpose flour, sifted
1$1/2$ cups ground almonds
4 tbsp heavy cream

14$1/2$ ounce can apricot
   halves, drained
1 cup fresh cranberries

1 To make the pie dough, place the flour and sugar in a bowl and rub in the butter with your fingers. Add the water and work the mixture together until a soft pie dough has formed. Wrap and chill for 30 minutes.

2 On a lightly floured surface, roll out the dough and line a 10-inch loose-bottomed quiche pan. Prick the dough with a fork and chill for 30 minutes.

3 Line the pie shell with foil and dried beans and bake in a preheated oven at 375°F for 15 minutes. Remove the foil and beans, return the pie shell to the oven and cook for a further 10 minutes.

4 To make the filling, cream together the butter and sugar until light and fluffy. Beat in the egg and egg yolks, then stir in the flour, almonds, and cream.

5 Place the apricot halves and cranberries on the bottom of the pie shell and spoon the filling over the top.

6 Bake in the oven for about 1 hour, or until the topping is just set. Cool slightly, then serve warm or cold.

White Chocolate & Almond Tart

*This is a variation on the classic pecan pie recipe—here nuts
and chocolate are encased in a thick syrup filling.*

Serves 8

INGREDIENTS

PIE DOUGH:
1¹/₄ cups all-purpose flour
5 tsp superfine sugar
¹/₂ cup butter, cut into
   small pieces
1 tbsp water

FILLING:
³/₄ cup light corn syrup
2 tbsp butter
¹/₃ cup light brown sugar
3 eggs, lightly beaten
¹/₂ cup whole blanched almonds,
   roughly chopped

3¹/₂ ounces white chocolate,
   roughly chopped
cream, to serve (optional)

1 To make the pie shell, place the flour and sugar in a mixing bowl and rub in the butter with your fingers. Add the water and work the mixture together until a soft pie dough has formed. Wrap and chill for 30 minutes.

2 On a lightly floured surface, roll out the dough and line a 10-inch loose-bottomed quiche pan. Prick the pie dough all over with a fork and chill for 30 minutes. Line the pie shell with foil and dried beans and bake in a preheated oven at 375°F for 15 minutes. Remove the foil and beans, return the pie shell to the oven and cook for a further 15 minutes.

3 To make the filling, gently melt the syrup, butter, and sugar together in a saucepan. Remove from the heat and let cool slightly. Add the beaten eggs, almonds, and chocolate, and stir until well blended.

4 Pour the chocolate and nut filling into the prepared pie shell and cook in the oven for 30–35 minutes, or until just set. Let cool before removing from the pan. Serve with cream, if desired.

VARIATION

You can use a mixture of white and dark chocolate, if preferred.

Mincemeat & Grape Jalousie

*This jalousie makes a good Christmastime dessert. Its festive
filling and flavor make it a great alternative to mince pies.*

Serves 4

INGREDIENTS

1 pound 2 ounces fresh ready-made
  puff pastry
14^1/$_2$ ounce jar mincemeat

3^1/$_2$ ounces grapes, seeded
  and halved
1 egg, for glazing

raw crystal sugar,
  for sprinkling

1 Lightly grease a cookie sheet with a little butter.

2 On a lightly floured surface, roll out the dough and cut it into 2 rectangles.

3 Place one dough rectangle onto the prepared cookie sheet and brush the edges with water.

4 Combine the mincemeat and grapes in a mixing bowl. Spread the mixture over the dough rectangle on the cookie sheet, leaving a 1-inch border all around.

5 Fold the second dough rectangle in half lengthwise. Using a sharp knife, carefully cut a series of parallel lines across the folded edge, leaving a 1-inch border.

6 Open out the puff pastry dough rectangle and lay it over the mincemeat. Seal down the edges of the dough and press together well.

7 Flute and crimp the edges of the dough. Lightly brush the dough with the beaten egg and sprinkle with a little raw crystal sugar.

8 Bake the jalousie in a preheated oven at 425°F for 15 minutes. Lower the heat to 350°F and cook for a further 30 minutes, until the jalousie is well risen and golden brown. Cool on a wire rack before serving.

COOK'S TIP

For an enhanced festive flavor, stir 2 tbsp sherry into the mincemeat.

Pear Tarts

These tarts are made with ready-made puff pastry which is available from most supermarkets. The finished pastry is rich and buttery.

Makes 6

INGREDIENTS

9 ounces fresh ready-made
   puff pastry
8 tsp light brown sugar

2 tbsp butter (plus extra
   for brushing)
1 tbsp finely chopped
   preserved ginger

3 pears, peeled, halved, and cored
cream, to serve

1 On a lightly floured surface, roll out the dough. Cut out six rounds 4 inches in diameter

2 Place the rounds on a large cookie sheet and chill for 30 minutes.

3 Cream together the brown sugar and butter in a small bowl, then stir in the chopped preserved ginger.

4 Prick the pastry rounds all over with a fork and spread a little of the ginger mixture onto each one.

5 Slice the pears halves lengthwise, keeping the pears intact at the tip. Carefully fan out the slices slightly.

6 Place a fanned-out pear half on top of each dough round. Make small flutes around the edge of the dough rounds and generously brush each pear half with melted butter.

7 Bake in a preheated oven at 400°F for 15–20 minutes, until the pastry is well risen and golden in color. Serve warm with a little cream.

COOK'S TIP

If you prefer, serve these tarts with vanilla ice cream for a delicious dessert.

Crème Brûlée Tarts

Serve these tarts with fresh fruit, if desired.

Makes 6

INGREDIENTS

PIE DOUGH:
1¼ cups all-purpose flour
5 tsp superfine sugar
½ cup butter, cut into
   small pieces.
1 tbsp water

FILLING:
4 egg yolks
¼ cup superfine sugar

1¾ cups heavy cream
1 tsp vanilla extract
raw crystal sugar,
   for sprinkling

1 To make the pie dough, place the flour and sugar in a large mixing bowl and rub in the butter with your fingertips. Add the water and work the mixture together until a soft pie dough has formed. Wrap and chill for 30 minutes.

2 On a lightly floured surface, roll out the dough to line six 4-inch tart pans. Prick the bottom of the pie dough all over with a fork and chill in the refrigerator for 20 minutes.

3 Line the pie shells with foil and dried beans and bake in a preheated oven at 375°F for 15 minutes. Remove the foil and beans and cook the pie shells for a further 10 minutes, until crisp and golden. Let cool.

4 Meanwhile, make the filling. In a bowl, beat the egg yolks and sugar until pale. Heat the cream and vanilla extract in a pan until just below boiling point, then pour it onto the egg mixture, whisking constantly.

5 Return the mixture to a clean pan and bring to just below a boil, stirring, until thick. Do not allow to boil or it will curdle.

6 Let the mixture cool slightly, then pour it into the tart pans. Cool and then chill overnight.

7 Sprinkle the tarts with the sugar. Place under a preheated broiler for a few minutes. Cool, then chill for 2 hours before serving.

Mini Frangipane Tarts with Lime

These little tartlets have an unusual limed-flavored pastry and are filled with an almond frangipane mixture.

Makes 12

INGREDIENTS

1 cup all-purpose flour	4 tbsp superfine sugar	$^1/_3$ cup confectioners' sugar, sifted
$^1/_3$ cup butter, softened	1 egg	$^1/_2$ tbsp water
1 tsp grated lime rind	$^1/_4$ cup ground almonds	
1 tbsp lime juice		

1 Reserve 5 teaspoons of the flour and 1 tablespoon of the butter and set aside until required.

2 Rub the remaining butter into the remaining flour, until the mixture resembles fine breadcrumbs. Stir in the lime rind, followed by the lime juice and bring the mixture together to form a soft dough.

3 On a lightly floured surface, roll out the dough thinly. Stamp out twelve 3-inch rounds and line a muffin pan.

4 In a bowl, cream together the reserved butter with the superfine sugar.

5 Mix in the egg, then the ground almonds and the reserved flour.

6 Divide the mixture between the pie shells.

7 Bake in a preheated oven at 400°F for 15 minutes, until set and lightly golden. Remove the tartlets from the pan and let cool.

8 Mix the confectioners' sugar with the water. Drizzle a little of the frosting over each tartlet and serve.

COOK'S TIP

These tartlets can be made in advance. Store them in an airtight container and ice them just before serving.

Breads & Side Dishes

Freshly baked bread has never been easier to make, especially with the easy blend yeasts available nowadays. In this chapter, packets containing 2 teaspoons of active dry yeast have been used, as it is easy to obtain, simple to use, and gives good results. If you want to use fresh yeast, replace one sachet of active dry yeast with 1 ounce of fresh yeast. Blend the fresh yeast into the warm liquid and add 1 teaspoon of sugar. Add to the flour and continue as usual.

Always choose a strong white or brown flour for the bread recipes using yeast, it contains a high proportion of gluten, the protein which gives the dough its elasticity. Always knead the dough thoroughly—this can be done in an electric mixer with the dough hook attachment for about 5–8 minutes, but kneading by hand is most enjoyable and satisfying.

This chapter also has a selection of side dishes to savor, including tasty pies, pastries, and flans to create a whole medley of delicious dishes that can be used as part of a main meal. Choose from Cheese Pudding, Onion Tart, and Fresh Tomato Tarts, and snacks like Mustard Scones and Curry Savory Biscuits.

Teacakes

These popular sweet snacks are ideal split in half and toasted, then spread with butter. Use a luxury mix of dried fruit containing candied cherries and apricots, and candied peel, if possible.

Serves 12

INGREDIENTS

4 cups strong white
  bread flour
1 packet active dry yeast
3 tbsp superfine sugar

1 tsp salt
2 tbsp butter, cut into
  small pieces
1¼ cups lukewarm milk

½ cup luxury dried fruit mix
honey, for brushing

1 Thoroughly grease several cookie sheets.

2 Sift the flour into a large mixing bowl. Stir in the yeast, sugar, and salt. Rub in the butter with your fingers until the mixture resembles fine breadcrumbs. Add the milk and mix all of the ingredients together to form a soft dough.

3 Place the dough on a lightly floured surface and knead for about 5 minutes (alternatively, you can knead the dough with an electric mixer with a dough hook).

4 Place the dough in a greased bowl, cover, and let rise in a warm place for 1–1½ hours, until it has doubled in size.

5 Knead the dough again for a few minutes and knead in the fruit. Divide the dough into 12 rounds and place on the cookie sheets. Cover and leave for a further 1 hour, or until springy to the touch.

6 Bake in a preheated oven at 400°F for 20 minutes. Brush the teacakes with honey while still warm.

7 Cool the teacakes on a wire rack before serving them split in half. Spread with butter and serve.

COOK'S TIP

It is important to have the milk at the right temperature: heat it until you can put your little finger into the milk and leave it there for 10 seconds without it feeling too hot.

Cinnamon Swirls

These cinnamon-flavored buns are delicious if they are served warm a few minutes after they come out of the oven.

Makes 12

INGREDIENTS

2 cups strong white
   bread flour
$1/2$ tsp salt
1 packet active dry yeast
2 tbsp butter, cut into
   small pieces

1 egg, beaten
$1/2$ cup warm milk
2 tbsp maple syrup

FILLING:
4 tbsp butter, softened
3 tbsp light brown sugar
2 tsp ground cinnamon
$1/3$ cup currants

1 Thoroughly grease a 9-inch square baking pan.

2 Sift the flour and salt into a mixing bowl. Stir in the yeast. Rub in the butter with your fingertips until the mixture resembles breadcrumbs. Add the egg and milk and mix everything to form a dough.

3 Place the dough in a greased bowl, cover, and leave in a warm place for about 40 minutes, or until doubled in size.

4 Knead the dough lightly for 1 minute to punch down, then roll out to a rectangle 12 x 9 inches.

5 To make the filling, cream together the butter, brown sugar, and cinnamon, until light and fluffy. Spread the filling over the dough, leaving a 1-inch border. Sprinkle the currants on top.

6 Roll up the dough like a jelly roll, from a long edge, and press to seal. Cut the roll into

12 slices. Place them in the pan, cover, and leave for 30 minutes.

7 Bake in a preheated oven at 375°F for 20–30 minutes, or until well risen. Brush with the syrup and cool slightly before serving.

VARIATION

If you prefer crunchy buns, replace the currants with chopped walnuts or pecans.

Cinnamon & Currant Loaf

This spicy, fruit tea bread is quick and easy to make. Serve it buttered and with a drizzle of honey for an afternoon snack.

Makes a 2-pound loaf

INGREDIENTS

3 cups all-purpose flour
pinch of salt
1 tbsp baking powder
1 tbsp ground cinnamon

$^2/_3$ cup butter, cut
  into small pieces
$^3/_4$ cup light brown sugar
$^3/_4$ cup currants

finely grated rind of 1 orange
5–6 tbsp orange juice
6 tbsp milk
2 eggs, lightly beaten

1 Thoroughly grease a 2-pound loaf pan and line the base with baking parchment.

2 Sift the flour, salt, baking powder, and ground cinnamon into a bowl. Rub in the butter pieces with your fingertips until the mixture resembles coarse breadcrumbs.

3 Stir in the sugar, currants, and orange rind. Beat the orange juice, milk, and eggs together and add to the dry ingredients. Mix well.

4 Spoon the mixture into the prepared pan. Make a slight dip in the middle of the mixture to help it rise evenly.

5 Bake in a preheated oven at 350°F for about 1–1 hour 10 minutes, or until a toothpick inserted into the center of the loaf comes out clean.

6 Let the loaf cool before turning out of the pan. Transfer to a wire rack and cool completely before slicing and serving.

COOK'S TIP

Once you have added the liquid to the dry ingredients, work as quickly as possible because the baking powder is activated by the liquid.

Orange, Banana, & Cranberry Loaf

The addition of chopped nuts, candied peel, fresh orange juice, and dried cranberries makes this a rich, moist tea bread.

Serves 8–10

INGREDIENTS

$1^1/_2$ cups self-rising flour
$^1/_2$ tsp baking powder
1 cup light brown sugar
2 bananas, mashed

1/4 cup chopped candied peel
1/4 cup chopped mixed nuts
1/2 cup dried cranberries
5–6 tbsp orange juice
2 eggs, beaten

$^2/_3$ cup sunflower oil
$^1/_3$ cup confectioners' sugar, sifted
grated rind of 1 orange

1 Thoroughly grease a 2-pound loaf pan and line the base with baking parchment.

2 Sift the flour and baking powder into a mixing bowl. Stir in the sugar, bananas, chopped candied peel, chopped nuts, and cranberries.

3 Stir the orange juice, eggs, and oil together until well combined. Add the mixture to the dry ingredients and mix until well blended. Pour the mixture into the prepared pan.

4 Bake in a preheated oven at 350°F for about 1 hour, until firm to the touch or until a toothpick inserted into the center of the loaf comes out clean.

6 Turn out the loaf and cool on a wire rack while you make the frosting.

7 Mix the confectioners' sugar with a little water and drizzle the frosting over the loaf. Sprinkle the orange rind over the top. Let the frosting set before serving the loaf in slices.

COOK'S TIP

This tea bread will keep for a couple of days. Wrap it carefully and store in a cool, dry place.

Banana & Date Loaf

This sweet bread is excellent served with coffee
with its moist texture and tempting flavor.

Serves 6–8

INGREDIENTS

2 cups self-rising flour
1/3 cup butter, cut into
    small pieces

1/3 cup superfine sugar
7/8 cup chopped, pitted dates
2 bananas, roughly mashed

2 eggs, lightly beaten
2 tbsp clear honey

1 Thoroughly grease a 2-pound loaf pan and line the base with baking parchment.

2 Sift the flour into a large mixing bowl.

3 Rub the butter into the flour with your fingertips until the mixture resembles fine breadcrumbs.

4 Stir the sugar, chopped dates, bananas, beaten eggs, and honey into the dry ingredients. Mix together to form a soft dropping consistency.

5 Spoon the mixture into the prepared loaf pan and level the surface with the back of a knife.

6 Bake in a preheated oven at 325°F for about 1 hour, or until golden and a toothpick inserted into the center comes out clean.

7 Let the loaf cool in the pan before turning out and transferring to a wire rack.

8 Serve the loaf warm or cold, cut into thick slices.

COOK'S TIP

This tea bread will keep for several days if stored in an airtight container and kept in a cool, dry place.

Crown Loaf

This is a rich sweet bread combining rum, nuts, and fruit in a decorative wreath shape. It is ideal for serving at Christmastime. You can omit the frosting and glaze with 2 tbsp honey, if preferred.

Makes 1 loaf

INGREDIENTS

2 cups strong white bread flour
$1/2$ tsp salt
1 packet active dry yeast
2 tbsp butter, cut into
   small pieces
$1/2$ cup lukewarm milk
1 egg, beaten

FILLING:
4 tbsp butter, softened
3 tbsp light brown sugar
1/4 cup chopped hazelnuts

2 tbsp chopped preserved ginger
$1/4$ cup candied peel
1 tbsp rum or brandy
$2/3$ cup confectioners' sugar
2 tbsp lemon juice

1 Grease a cookie sheet. Sift the flour and salt into a bowl. Stir in the yeast. Rub in the butter with your fingers. Add the milk and egg and mix together to form a dough.

2 Place the dough in a greased bowl, cover, and leave in a warm place for 40 minutes, until doubled in size. Knead the dough lightly for 1 minute to punch down. Roll out to a rectangle 12 x 9 inches.

3 To make the filling, cream together the butter and sugar until light and fluffy. Stir in the hazelnuts, ginger, candied peel, and rum or brandy. Spread the filling over the dough, leaving a 1-inch border.

4 Roll up the dough, starting from the long edge, to form a sausage shape. Cut into slices at 2-inch intervals and place on the cookie sheet in a circle with the slices just touching. Cover and let

rise in a warm place for 30 minutes.

5 Bake in a preheated oven at 325°F for 20–30 minutes, or until golden. Meanwhile, mix the confectioners' sugar with enough lemon juice to form a thin frosting.

6 Let the loaf cool slightly before drizzling the whole circle with frosting. Allow to set slightly before serving the loaf.

Date & Honey Loaf

This bread is full of good things—chopped dates, sesame seeds, and honey.
Toast thick slices and spread with soft cheese for a light snack.

Makes 1 loaf

INGREDIENTS

1^1/$_4$ cups strong white bread flour
^{1}/$_4$ cup strong brown bread flour

^{1}/$_2$ tsp salt
1 packet active dry yeast
^{3}/$_4$ cup lukewarm water
3 tbsp sunflower oil

3 tbsp honey
^{1}/$_2$ cup chopped, pitted dates
2 tbsp sesame seeds

1 Grease a 2-pound loaf pan. Sift the flours into a large mixing bowl, stir in the salt and yeast.

2 Pour in the water, oil, and honey. Mix everything together to form a dough.

3 Place the dough on a lightly floured surface and knead for about 5 minutes, until smooth.

4 Place the dough in a greased bowl, cover, and let rise in a warm place for about 1 hour, or until doubled in size.

5 Knead in the dates and sesame seeds. Shape the dough and place in the pan.

6 Cover and leave in a warm place for a further 30 minutes, or until springy to the touch.

7 Bake in a preheated oven at 425°F for 30 minutes, or until a hollow sound can be heard when the base of the loaf is tapped with the knuckles.

8 Transfer the loaf to a wire rack and let cool. Serve cut into thick slices.

VARIATION

Replace the sesame seeds with sunflower seeds for a slightly different texture, if you prefer.

COOK'S TIP

If you cannot find a warm place, sit a bowl with the dough in it over a saucepan of warm water and cover.

Pumpkin Loaf

The pumpkin purée in this loaf makes it beautifully moist.
It is delicious eaten at any time of the day.

Serves 6–8

INGREDIENTS

3¹/₂ cups chopped pumpkin flesh
¹/₂ cup butter, softened
³/₄ cup superfine sugar
2 eggs, beaten
2 cups all-purpose flour, sifted

1¹/₂ tsp baking powder
¹/₂ tsp salt
1 tsp ground apple pie spice
1/3 cup pumpkin seeds

1 Grease a 2-pound loaf pan with oil.

2 Wrap the pumpkin pieces in buttered foil. Cook in a preheated oven at 400°F for 30–40 minutes, until they are cooked through and tender.

3 Let the pumpkin cool completely before mashing well to make a thick purée.

4 In a bowl, cream the butter and sugar together until light and fluffy. Add the eggs, a little at a time.

5 Stir in the pumpkin purée. Fold in the flour, baking powder, salt, and apple pie spice.

6 Fold the pumpkin seeds gently through the mixture. Spoon the mixture into the prepared loaf pan.

7 Bake in a preheated oven at 325°F for approximately 1¹/₄–1¹/₂ hours, or until a toothpick inserted into the center of the loaf comes out clean.

8 Let the loaf cool and serve buttered, if desired.

COOK'S TIP

To ensure that the pumpkin purée is dry, place it in a saucepan over a medium heat for a few minutes, stirring frequently, until it is thick.

Tropical Fruit Bread

The ginger, coconut, and pineapple flavors in this bread will bring an instant touch of sunshine to your breakfast table. The mango can be replaced with any other dried fruit or orange rind.

Makes 1 loaf

INGREDIENTS

3 cups strong white bread flour
5 tbsp bran
$\frac{1}{2}$ tsp salt
$\frac{1}{2}$ tsp ground ginger
1 packet active dry yeast
2 tbsp light brown sugar

2 tbsp butter, cut into
    small pieces
generous 1 cup lukewarm water
$\frac{1}{2}$ cup finely chopped,
    candied pineapple

3 tbsp finely chopped dried mango
$\frac{2}{3}$ cup shredded coconut, toasted
1 egg, beaten
2 tbsp coconut shreds

1 Thoroughly grease a cookie sheet. Sift the flour into a large mixing bowl. Stir in the bran, salt, ginger, yeast, and sugar. Rub in the butter with your fingers, then add the water, and mix to form a dough.

2 On a lightly floured surface, knead the dough for about 5–8 minutes, or until smooth (alternatively, use an electric mixer with a dough hook). Place the dough in a greased bowl, cover, and let rise in a warm place until doubled in size.

3 Knead the candied pineapple, dried mango, and shredded coconut into the dough. Shape into a round loaf and place on the cookie sheet. Score the top with the back of a knife. Cover and leave for a further 30 minutes in a warm place.

4 Brush the loaf with the egg and sprinkle with the 2 tbsp coconut. Bake in a preheated oven at 425°F for 30 minutes, or until golden in color.

5 Let the bread cool on a wire rack before serving.

COOK'S TIP

To test the bread after the second rising, gently poke the dough with your finger—it should spring back if it has risen enough.

Citrus Bread

This sweet loaf is flavored with citrus fruits. As with
Tropical Fruit Bread (see page 80), it is excellent served at breakfast.

Makes 1 loaf

INGREDIENTS

4 cups strong white bread flour
$^1/_2$ tsp salt
$^1/_4$ cup superfine sugar
1 packet active dry yeast
4 tbsp butter, cut into small pieces
5–6 tbsp orange juice
4 tbsp lemon juice

3–4 tbsp lime juice
$^2/_3$ cup lukewarm water
1 orange
1 lemon
1 lime
2 tbsp clear honey

1 Lightly grease a cookie sheet.

2 Sift the flour and salt into a mixing bowl. Stir in the sugar and yeast.

3 Rub the butter into the mixture using your fingers. Add all of the fruit juices and the water and mix to form a dough.

4 Place the dough on a lightly floured counter and knead

for 5 minutes (alternatively, use an electric mixer with a dough hook). Place the dough in a greased bowl, cover, and let rise in a warm place for 1 hour.

5 Meanwhile, grate the rind of the orange, lemon, and lime. Knead the fruit rinds into the dough.

6 Divide the dough into 2 balls, making one slightly bigger than the other.

7 Place the larger ball on the cookie sheet and set the smaller one on top.

8 Push a floured finger through the center of the dough. Cover and let rise for about 40 minutes or until springy to the touch.

9 Bake in a preheated oven at 425°F for 35 minutes. Remove from the oven and glaze with the honey.

Mango Twist Bread

This is a sweet bread which has puréed mango mixed into the dough,
resulting in a moist loaf with an exotic flavor.

Makes 1 loaf

INGREDIENTS

4 cups strong white bread flour
1 tsp salt
1 packet active dry yeast
1 tsp ground ginger
3 tbsp light brown sugar
3 tbsp butter, cut into small pieces

1 small mango, peeled, cored,
 and puréed
generous 1 cup lukewarm water
2 tbsp clear honey
$^2/_3$ cup golden raisins

1 egg, beaten
confectioners' sugar,
 for dusting

1 Thoroughly grease a cookie sheet. Sift the flour and salt into a large mixing bowl and stir in the yeast, ground ginger, and brown sugar. Rub in the butter with your fingers.

2 Stir in the mango purée, water, and honey and mix together to form a dough.

3 Place the dough on a lightly floured surface and knead for about 5 minutes, until smooth (alternatively, use an electric mixer with a dough hook). Place the dough in a greased bowl, cover, and let rise in a warm place for about 1 hour, until it has doubled in size.

4 Knead in the golden raisins and shape the dough into 2 sausage shapes, each 10 inches long. Carefully twist the 2 pieces together and pinch the ends to seal. Place the dough on the cookie sheet, cover and let rise in a warm place for a further 40 minutes.

5 Brush the loaf with the egg and bake in a preheated oven, at 425°F for 30 minutes, or until golden brown. Leave on a wire rack to cool completely. Dust with confectioners' sugar before serving.

COOK'S TIP

You can tell when the bread is cooked as it will sound hollow when tapped on the bottom.

Chocolate Bread

For the chocoholics among us, this bread is fun to make and even better to eat.

Makes 1 loaf

INGREDIENTS

4 cups strong white bread flour
1/4 cup unsweetened cocoa

1 tsp salt
1 packet active dry yeast
2 tbsp light brown sugar

1 tbsp oil
1 1/2 cups lukewarm water

1 Lightly grease a 2-pound loaf pan.

2 Sift the flour and the unsweetened cocoa into a large mixing bowl.

3 Stir in the salt, yeast, and brown sugar.

4 Pour in the oil along with the water and mix the ingredients together to make a dough.

5 Place the dough on a lightly floured surface and knead for 5 minutes.

6 Place the dough in a greased bowl, cover, and let rise in a warm place for about 1 hour, or until the dough has doubled in size.

7 Punch down the dough and shape it into a loaf. Place the dough into the prepared pan, cover, and then let rise in a warm place for a further 30 minutes.

8 Bake in a preheated oven at 400°F for 25–30 minutes, or until a hollow sound can be heard when the base of the bread is tapped.

9 Transfer the bread to a wire rack and cool. Cut into slices to serve.

COOK'S TIP

This bread can be sliced and spread with butter or it can be lightly toasted.

Soda Bread

*This variation of traditional Irish soda bread is best
eaten the same day it has been baked.*

Makes 1 loaf

INGREDIENTS

2½ cups whole-wheat flour
2½ cups all-purpose flour

2 tsp baking powder
1 tsp baking soda
2 tbsp superfine sugar

1 tsp salt
1 egg, beaten
1¾ cups unsweetened yogurt

1 Thoroughly grease and flour a cookie sheet.

2 Sift the flours, baking powder, baking soda, sugar, and salt into a large bowl.

3 In a mixing bowl, beat together the egg and yogurt and pour the mixture into the dry ingredients. Mix everything together to make a soft and sticky dough.

4 On a lightly floured surface, knead the dough for a few minutes until it is smooth, then shape the dough into a round loaf about 2 inches deep.

5 Transfer the dough to the cookie sheet. Mark a cross shape in the center of the top of the dough.

6 Bake in a preheated oven at 375°F for about 40 minutes, or until the bread is a golden brown color.

7 Transfer the loaf to a wire rack and cool slightly before serving. Cut into slices to serve.

VARIATION

For a delicious fruity version of this soda bread, add ¾ cup of raisins to the dry ingredients in step 2.

Spicy Bread

*Serve this spicy bread fresh from the oven with your
favorite soup for a light lunch or supper.*

Makes 1 loaf

INGREDIENTS

2 cups self-rising flour
³/₄ cup all-purpose flour

1 tsp baking powder
¹/₄ tsp salt
¹/₄ tsp cayenne pepper
2 tsp curry powder

2 tsp poppy seeds
2 tbsp butter, cut into small pieces
²/₃ cup milk
1 egg, beaten

1 Thoroughly grease a cookie sheet with butter.

2 Sift the self-rising flour and the all-purpose flour into a large mixing bowl, together with the baking powder, salt, cayenne pepper, curry powder, and poppy seeds.

3 Rub in the butter with your fingers until everything is well mixed together.

4 Add the milk and the beaten egg and mix to a soft dough.

5 Turn the dough out onto a lightly floured surface, then knead the dough lightly for a few minutes.

6 Shape the dough into a round loaf and mark it with a cross shape in the center of the top of the dough.

7 Bake in a preheated oven at 375°F for 45 minutes.

8 Transfer the bread to a wire rack and let cool. Serve in chunks or slices.

COOK'S TIP

*If the bread looks as though it is
browning too much, cover it with
a piece of foil for the remainder
of the cooking time.*

Chili Corn Bread

*This Mexican-style corn bread makes a great accompaniment
to chili or it can be eaten on its own as a tasty snack.*

Makes 12 bars

INGREDIENTS

1 cup all-purpose flour
1 cup cornmeal
1 tbsp baking powder
$^1/_2$ tsp salt

1 green chili, seeded and
  finely chopped
5 scallions, finely chopped
2 eggs

generous $^1/_2$ cup sour cream
$^1/_2$ cup sunflower oil

1 Grease an 8-inch square cake pan and line the base with baking parchment.

2 In a large bowl, mix the flour, cornmeal, baking powder, and salt together.

3 Add the finely chopped green chili, and the scallions to the dry ingredients and mix well.

4 In a large mixing bowl, beat the eggs, together with the sour cream and sunflower oil. Pour the mixture into the bowl

of dry ingredients. Mix all of the ingredients together quickly and thoroughly.

5 Pour the mixture into the prepared cake pan.

6 Bake in a preheated oven at 400°F for 20–25 minutes, or until the loaf has risen and is lightly browned.

7 Let the bread cool slightly before turning out of the pan. Cut into bars or squares to serve.

VARIATION
*Add $^3/_4$ cup of corn kernels to the
mixture in step 3,
if you prefer.*

Cheese & Potato Bread

This lovely cheesy bread is ideal for a quick savory snack.
The mashed potato gives it a deliciously moist texture.

Serves 4

INGREDIENTS

2 cups all-purpose flour
1 tsp salt

$^1/_2$ tsp mustard powder
2 tsp baking powder
1 cup grated Red Leicester cheese

2 cups cooked, mashed potatoes
$^3/_4$ cup water
1 tbsp oil

1 Lightly grease a cookie sheet.

2 Sift the flour, salt, mustard powder, and baking powder into a mixing bowl.

3 Reserve 2 tbsp of the grated cheese and stir the rest into the bowl with the cooked and mashed potatoes.

4 Pour in the water and the oil, and stir all the ingredients together (the mixture will be wet at this stage). Mix them all to make a soft dough.

5 Turn out the dough onto a floured surface and shape it into an 8-inch round loaf.

6 Place the loaf on the cookie sheet and mark it into 4 portions with a knife, without cutting through. Sprinkle with the reserved cheese.

7 Bake in a preheated oven at 425°F for approximately 25–30 minutes.

8 Transfer the bread to a wire rack and let cool. Serve the bread as fresh as possible.

COOK'S TIP

You can use instant potato mix for this bread, if you prefer.

VARIATION

Add $^1/_3$ cup chopped ham to the mixture in step 3, if you prefer.

Cheese & Ham Loaf

This recipe is a quick way to make tasty bread, using self-rising flour and baking powder to ensure a good rising. Once you have added the liquid ingredients, you need to work quickly.

Serves 6

INGREDIENTS

2 cups self-rising flour
1 tsp salt
2 tsp baking powder

1 tsp paprika
$^1/_3$ cup butter, cut into small pieces
1 cup grated sharp cheese

$^1/_2$ cup smoked ham, chopped
2 eggs, beaten
$^2/_3$ cup milk

1 Thoroughly grease a 1-pound loaf pan and line the base with baking parchment.

2 Sift the flour, salt, baking powder, and paprika into a mixing bowl.

3 Rub in the butter with your fingers until the mixture resembles fine breadcrumbs. Stir in the cheese and ham.

4 Add the beaten eggs and milk to the dry ingredients in the bowl and combine well.

5 Spoon the cheese and ham mixture into the prepared loaf pan.

6 Bake the mixture in a preheated oven at 350°F for about 1 hour, or until the loaf is well risen.

7 Let the bread cool in the pan, then turn out, and transfer to a wire rack to cool completely.

8 Serve the bread cut into thick slices.

COOK'S TIP

This tasty bread is best eaten on the day it is made, as it does not keep well for very long.

VARIATION

Any grated hard cheese can be used for this bread; use a milder one, if preferred.

Cheese & Chive Bread

*This is a quick bread to make. It is fully of cheesy flavor and,
to enjoy it at its best, it should be eaten as fresh as possible.*

Serves 8

INGREDIENTS

2 cups self-rising flour
1 tsp salt
1 tsp mustard powder

1 cup grated sharp cheese
2 tbsp chopped fresh chives
1 egg, beaten

2 tbsp butter, melted
$^{2}/_{3}$ cup milk

1 Grease a 9-inch square cake pan and line the base with baking parchment.

2 Sift the flour, salt, and mustard powder into a large mixing bowl.

3 Reserve 3 tbsp of the grated sharp cheese for sprinkling over the top of the loaf before baking in the oven.

4 Stir the remaining cheese into the bowl, together with the chopped fresh chives. Mix well.

5 Add the beaten egg, melted butter, and milk and stir the mixture thoroughly.

6 Pour the mixture into the prepared pan and spread with a knife. Sprinkle with the reserved grated cheese.

7 Bake in a preheated oven at 375°F for about 30 minutes.

8 Let the bread cool slightly in the pan. Turn out the bread onto a wire rack to cool further before serving. Cut into triangles to serve.

COOK'S TIP

You can use any hard sharp cheese of your choice for this recipe.

Garlic Bread Rolls

This bread is not at all like the store-bought, ready-made garlic bread.
Instead it has a subtle flavor and a soft texture.

Makes 8

INGREDIENTS

12 cloves garlic, peeled
1¹/₂ cups milk
4 cups strong white
   bread flour

1 tsp salt
1 packet active dry yeast
1 tbsp dried mixed herbs
2 tbsp sunflower oil

1 egg, beaten
milk, for brushing
rock salt, for sprinkling

1 Grease a cookie sheet. Place the garlic cloves and milk in a saucepan, bring to a boil, and simmer gently for 15 minutes. Cool slightly, then process in a blender or food processor to purée the garlic.

2 Sift the flour and the 1 teaspoon of salt into a large mixing bowl and stir in the yeast and mixed herbs.

3 Add the garlic-flavored milk, sunflower oil, and beaten egg to the dry ingredients and mix everything to a dough.

4 Place the dough on a lightly floured counter and knead lightly for a few minutes until smooth and soft.

5 Place the dough in a greased bowl, cover, and let rise in a warm place for about 1 hour, or until doubled in size.

6 Punch down the dough by kneading it vigorously for 2 minutes. Shape into 8 rolls and place on the prepared cookie sheet. Lightly score the top of each roll with a knife, cover, and leave for 15 minutes.

7 Brush the rolls with a little milk and sprinkle rock salt over the top.

8 Bake in a preheated oven at 425°F for 15–20 minutes.

9 Transfer the rolls to a wire rack and cool completely before serving.

COOK'S TIP

Sprinkle the rolls with 1 clove of finely chopped garlic in step 7, if you prefer.

Mini Focaccia

This is a delicious Italian bread made with olive oil.

Makes 4

INGREDIENTS

3 cups strong white flour
$\frac{1}{2}$ tsp salt
1 packet active dry yeast
2 tbsp olive oil

$1\frac{1}{8}$ cups lukewarm water
1 cup pitted green or black
  olives, halved

TOPPING:
2 red onions, sliced
2 tbsp olive oil
1 tsp sea salt
1 tbsp thyme leaves

1 Lightly oil several cookie sheets. Sift the flour and salt into a large mixing bowl, then stir in the yeast. Pour in the olive oil and water and mix everything together to form a dough.

2 Turn the dough out onto a lightly floured surface and knead it for about 10 minutes (alternatively, use an electric mixer with a dough hook and knead for 7–8 minutes).

3 Place the dough in a greased bowl, cover, and leave in a warm place for about 1–1$\frac{1}{2}$ hours, until it has doubled in size. Punch down the dough by kneading it again for 1–2 minutes.

4 Knead half of the olives into the dough. Divide the dough into quarters and then shape the quarters into rounds. Place them on the cookie sheets and push your fingers into the dough to achieve a dimpled effect.

5 To make the topping, sprinkle the red onions and remaining olives over the rounds. Drizzle the olive oil over the top and sprinkle each round with the sea salt and thyme leaves. Cover and let the dough rise again for 30 minutes.

6 Bake in a preheated oven at 375°F for 20–25 minutes, or until the focaccia are well cooked and golden.

7 Transfer to a wire rack and cool before serving.

VARIATION

Use this quantity of dough to make 1 large focaccia, if you prefer.

Sun-dried Tomato Rolls

These white rolls have the addition of finely chopped sun-dried tomatoes.
The tomatoes are sold in jars and are readily available at most supermarkets.

Makes 8

INGREDIENTS

2 cups strong white
   bread flour
$1/2$ tsp salt
1 packet active dry yeast

$1/3$ cup butter, melted and
   cooled slightly
3 tbsp milk, warmed
2 eggs, beaten

1 cup drained and finely chopped
   sun-dried tomatoes
milk, for brushing

1 Lightly grease a cookie sheet with a little butter.

2 Sift the flour and salt into a large mixing bowl. Stir in the yeast, then pour in the butter, milk, and eggs. Mix together to form a dough.

3 Turn the dough onto a lightly floured surface and knead for about 5 minutes (alternatively, use an electric mixer with a dough hook).

4 Place the dough in a greased bowl, cover, and let rise in a warm place for 1–1$1/2$ hours, until the dough has doubled in size. Punch down the dough by kneading it lightly for a few minutes.

5 Knead the sun-dried tomatoes into the dough, sprinkling the counter with extra flour as the tomatoes are quite oily.

6 Divide the dough into 8 balls and place them on the prepared cookie sheet. Cover and let rise for about 30 minutes, until the rolls have doubled in size.

7 Lightly brush the rolls with a little milk and bake in a preheated oven, at 450°F for 10–15 minutes, until the rolls are golden brown.

8 Transfer the rolls to a wire rack and cool slightly before serving.

COOK'S TIP

The active dry yeast used in this recipe is widely available in most supermarkets.

Thyme Crescents

These savory crescent snacks are very similar to croissants and are perfect for a quick and tasty bite to eat. They can also be shaped into twists, if preferred.

Makes 8

INGREDIENTS

9 ounces fresh ready-made puff
   pastry
1/3 cup butter, softened

1 garlic clove, crushed
1 tsp lemon juice
1 tsp dried thyme

salt and pepper

1 Lightly grease a cookie sheet with a little butter.

2 On a lightly floured surface, roll out the pastry dough to form a 10-inch round and cut into 8 wedges.

3 In a small bowl, mix the softened butter, garlic clove, lemon juice, and dried thyme together until soft. Season with salt and pepper to taste.

4 Spread a little of the butter and thyme mixture onto each wedge of pastry dough, dividing it equally between them.

5 Carefully roll up each wedge of pastry dough, starting from the wide end.

6 Arrange the crescents on the prepared cookie sheet and chill for 30 minutes.

7 Dampen the cookie sheet with cold water. This will create a steamy atmosphere in the oven while the crescents are baking and help the pastries to rise.

8 Bake in a preheated oven at 400°F for 10–15 minutes, until the crescents are well risen and golden.

COOK'S TIP

Dried herbs have a stronger flavor than fresh ones, which makes them perfect for these pastries. The crescents can be made with other dried herbs of your choice, such as rosemary and sage, or mixed herbs.

Cheese & Mustard Scones

These homemade scones are given an interesting flavor by adding grated sharp cheese and mustard to the mixture.

Makes 8

INGREDIENTS

2 cups self-rising flour
1 tsp baking powder
pinch of salt

$^1/_3$ cup butter, cut into small pieces
1 cup grated sharp cheese
1 tsp mustard powder

$^2/_3$ cup milk
pepper

1 Lightly grease a cookie sheet.

2 Sift the flour, baking powder, and salt into a mixing bowl. Rub in the butter with your fingers until the mixture resembles breadcrumbs.

3 Stir in the grated cheese, mustard, and enough milk to form a soft dough.

4 On a lightly floured surface, knead the dough very lightly, then flatten it out with the palm of your hand to a depth of about 1 inch.

5 Cut the dough into 8 wedges with a knife. Brush each one with a little milk and sprinkle with pepper to taste.

6 Bake in a preheated oven at 425°F for 10–15 minutes, until the scones are a golden brown color.

7 Transfer the scones to a wire rack and cool slightly before serving.

COOK'S TIP

Scones should be eaten on the day they are made, as they quickly go stale. Serve them split in half and spread with butter.

Cheese Sables

*These savory crackers have a delicious buttery flavor. Make sure
you use a sharp cheese for the best flavor.*

Makes about 35

INGREDIENTS

1$\frac{1}{4}$ cups all-purpose flour
1$\frac{1}{2}$ cup grated sharp cheese

$\frac{2}{3}$ cup butter, cut into
  small pieces
1 egg yolk

sesame seeds, for sprinkling

1 Lightly grease several cookie
sheets.

2 Mix the flour and cheese
together in a bowl.

3 Add the butter to the cheese
and flour mixture and mix
with your fingers until combined.

4 Stir in the egg yolk and mix
to form a dough. Wrap the
dough and chill in the refrigerator
for about 30 minutes.

5 On a lightly floured surface,
roll out the cheese dough

thinly. Cut out 2$\frac{1}{2}$-inch rounds,
re-rolling the trimmings to make
about 35 rounds.

6 Place the rounds onto the
prepared cookie sheets and
sprinkle the sesame seeds over the
top of them.

7 Bake in a preheated oven
at 400°F for 20 minutes,
until the sables are a light golden
color.

8 Transfer the cheese sables to a
wire rack and cool slightly
before serving.

COOK'S TIP

*Cut out any shape you like
for your savory crackers. Children
will enjoy them cut into animal or
other fun shapes.*

Savory Curried Crackers

*When making these crackers, try different types of curry powder
strengths until you find the one that suits your own tastes.*

Makes 40

INGREDIENTS

$^3/_4$ cup all-purpose flour
1 tsp salt
2 tsp curry powder

1 cup grated mellow hard cheese
1 cup grated Parmesan cheese

$^1/_3$ cup butter, softened

1 Lightly grease about 4 cookie sheets.

2 Sift the all-purpose flour and salt into a mixing bowl.

3 Stir in the curry powder, the grated mellow hard cheese, and the grated Parmesan cheese. Rub in the softened butter with your fingertips until the mixture comes together to form a soft dough.

4 On a lightly floured surface, roll out the dough thinly to form a rectangle.

5 Using a 2-inch cutter, cut out 40 round biscuits.

6 Arrange the biscuits on the cookie sheets.

7 Bake in a preheated oven at 350°F for 10–15 minutes.

8 Let the biscuits cool slightly on the cookie sheets.

9 Transfer the biscuits to a wire rack until completely cold and crisp, then serve.

COOK'S TIP

*These crackers can be stored for
several days in an airtight metal or
plastic container.*

Cheese Pudding

This savory cheese pudding is very like a soufflé in texture, but it does not rise like a traditional soufflé.

Serves 4

INGREDIENTS

$2^{1}/_{2}$ cups fresh white breadcrumbs
1 cup grated Swiss cheese

$^{2}/_{3}$ cup lukewarm milk
$^{1}/_{2}$ cup butter, melted
2 eggs, separated

2 tbsp chopped fresh parsley
salt and pepper
salad greens, to serve

1 Thoroughly grease a 5 cup ovenproof dish.

2 Place the breadcrumbs and cheese in a bowl and mix.

3 Pour the milk over the cheese and breadcrumb mixture and stir to mix. Add the melted butter, egg yolks, parsley, and salt and pepper to taste. Mix well.

4 Whisk the egg whites until firm. Fold the cheese mixture into the egg whites.

5 Transfer the mixture to the prepared ovenproof dish.

6 Bake the pudding in a preheated oven at 375°F for about 45 minutes or until golden brown, and slightly risen, and a knife inserted into the middle of the pudding comes out clean.

7 Serve the cheese pudding hot, with salad greens.

VARIATION

Any strongly flavored cheese of your choice can be used instead of the Swiss cheese to make this tasty savory pudding.

COOK'S TIP

For a slightly healthier alternative, make the cheese pudding with fresh whole-wheat breadcrumbs instead of white ones.

Cheese & Onion Pies

These crisp pies are filled with a tasty onion, garlic, and parsley mixture, making them ideal for picnics.

Makes 4

INGREDIENTS

3 tbsp vegetable oil
4 onions, peeled and finely sliced
4 garlic cloves, crushed
4 tbsp finely chopped fresh
  parsley
$^3/_4$ cup grated sharp cheese
salt and pepper

PIE DOUGH:
$1^1/_2$ cups all-purpose flour
$^1/_2$ tsp salt

$^1/_3$ cup butter, cut into
  small pieces
3–4 tbsp water

1 Heat the oil in a skillet. Add the onions and garlic and sauté for 10–15 minutes, or until the onions are soft. Remove the pan from the heat and stir in the parsley and cheese, and season.

2 To make the pie dough, sift the flour and salt into a mixing bowl and rub in the butter with your fingertips until the mixture resembles breadcrumbs. Stir in the water and mix to a smooth dough.

3 On a lightly floured surface, roll out the dough and divide it into 8 portions.

4 Roll out each portion to a 4-inch round and use half of the rounds to line 4 individual tart pans.

5 Fill each round with a quarter of the onion mixture. Cover with the remaining 4 pie dough rounds. Make a slit in the top of each pie with the point of a knife and seal the edges with the back of a teaspoon.

6 Bake in a preheated oven at 425°F for 20 minutes. Serve hot or cold.

COOK'S TIP

You can prepare the onion filling in advance and store it in the refrigerator until required.

Red Onion Tart Tatin

*Ready-made puff pie dough works extremely well in this recipe
and means you create a delicious savory tart in very little time.*

Serves 4

INGREDIENTS

4 tbsp butter

2 tbsp sugar

1 pound 2 ounces red onions, peeled
   and quartered

3 tbsp red wine vinegar

2 tbsp fresh thyme leaves

8 ounces fresh ready-made puff
   pastry

salt and pepper

1 Place the butter and sugar in
a 9-inch ovenproof skillet and
cook over a medium heat until the
butter has melted.

2 Add the red onion quarters
and sweat them over a low
heat for 10–15 minutes, until
golden, stirring occasionally.

3 Add the red wine vinegar and
thyme leaves to the skillet.
Season with salt and pepper to
taste, then simmer over a medium
heat until the liquid has reduced
and the red onion pieces are
coated in the buttery sauce.

4 On a lightly floured kitchen
counter, roll out the pastry to
a round slightly larger than the
skillet.

5 Place the dough over the
onion mixture and press
down, tucking in the edges to seal
the pie dough.

6 Bake in a preheated oven at
350°F for 20–25 minutes. Let
the tart stand for 10 minutes.

7 To turn out, place a serving
plate over the skillet and
carefully invert them both so that

the dough crust becomes
the base of the tart. Serve the
tart warm.

VARIATION

*Replace the red onions with
shallots, leaving them whole,
if you prefer.*

Puff Potato Pie

*This pie with its rich filling is a great alternative to serving potatoes
as a side dish with any meal. Alternatively, serve with salad for a light lunch.*

Serves 6

INGREDIENTS

1 pound 9 ounces potatoes, peeled
and thinly sliced
2 scallions, finely chopped

1 red onion, finely chopped
²/₃ cup heavy cream

1 pound 2 ounces fresh ready-made
puff pastry
2 eggs, beaten
salt and pepper

1 Lightly grease a cookie sheet. Bring a saucepan of water to a boil, add the sliced potatoes, bring back to a boil, and then simmer for a few minutes. Drain the potato slices and cool. Dry off any excess moisture with paper towels.

2 In a bowl, mix together the scallions, red onion, and the cooled potato slices. Stir in 2 tablespoons of the cream and plenty of seasoning.

3 Divide the pastry in half and roll out one piece to a 9-inch round. Roll the remaining dough to a 10-inch round.

4 Place the smaller round onto the cookie sheet and top with the potato mixture, leaving a 1-inch border all around. Brush this border with a little of the beaten egg.

5 Top with the larger round of dough, seal well, and crimp the edges of the dough. Cut a steam vent in the middle of the dough and, using the back of a knife, mark with a pattern. Brush with the beaten egg and bake in a preheated oven at 400°F for 30 minutes.

6 Mix the remaining beaten egg with the rest of the cream and pour into the pie through the steam vent. Return the pie to the oven for 15 minutes, then let cool for 30 minutes. Serve either warm or cold.

COOK'S TIP

*The filling may be prepared up to
4 hours in advance.*

Fresh Tomato Tarts

*These tomato-flavored tarts should be eaten as fresh as possible
to enjoy the light and crisp buttery puff crust.*

Serves 6

INGREDIENTS

9 ounces fresh ready-made puff
  pastry
1 egg, beaten

2 tbsp pesto
6 plum tomatoes, sliced
salt and pepper

fresh thyme leaves, to garnish
  (optional)

1 On a lightly floured kitchen counter, roll out the pastry dough to a rectangle measuring 12 x 10 inches.

2 Cut the rectangle in half and divide each half into 3 pieces to make 6 even-size rectangles. Chill for 20 minutes.

3 Lightly score the edges of the dough rectangles and brush with the beaten egg.

4 Spread the pesto over the rectangles, dividing it equally between them, leaving a 1-inch border on each one.

5 Arrange the tomato slices along the center of each rectangle on top of the pesto.

6 Season well with salt and pepper to taste and lightly sprinkle with fresh thyme leaves, if using.

7 Bake in a preheated oven at 400°F for 15–20 minutes, until well risen and a golden brown color.

8 Transfer the tomato tarts to warm serving plates straight from the oven and serve while they are still piping hot.

VARIATION

Instead of making individual tarts, roll the dough out to form 1 large rectangle. Spoon the pesto on and arrange the tomatoes over the top.

Provençal Tart

*This tart is full of color and flavor from the zucchini and red
and green bell peppers. It makes a great change from a quiche Lorraine.*

Serves 6–8

INGREDIENTS

9 ounces ready-made fresh puff
  pastry
3 tbsp olive oil
2 red bell peppers, seeded and diced

2 green bell peppers, seeded
  and diced
$2/3$ cup heavy cream

1 egg
2 zucchini, sliced
salt and pepper

1 Roll out the pastry on a
lightly floured surface and
line an 8-inch loose-bottomed
quiche pan. Chill in the
refrigerator for 20 minutes.

2 Meanwhile, heat 2 tbsp of the
olive oil in a skillet and sauté
the bell peppers for about
8 minutes, until softened,
stirring frequently.

3 Whisk the heavy cream and
egg together in a bowl and
season to taste with salt and
pepper. Stir in the cooked mixed
bell peppers.

4 Heat the remaining oil in a
pan and fry the zucchini slices
for 4–5 minutes, until they are
lightly browned.

5 Carefully pour the egg and
bell pepper mixture into the
pie shell.

6 Arrange the zucchini slices in
a pattern around the edge of
the tart.

7 Bake in a preheated oven at
350°F for 35–40 minutes, or
until just set and golden brown.
Serve hot or cold.

COOK'S TIP

*This recipe could be used to make
6 individual tarts—use 6 x 4 inch
pans and bake them for
20 minutes.*

Celery & Onion Pies

*These savory celery and onion pies are quite irresistible,
so it is probably a good idea to bake a double batch!*

Makes 12

INGREDIENTS

PIE DOUGH:
1 cup all-purpose flour
1/2 tsp salt
2 tbsp butter, cut into
 small pieces

1/4 cup grated sharp cheese
3–4 tbsp water

FILLING:
4 tbsp butter
1 cup finely chopped celery
2 garlic cloves, crushed

1 small onion, finely chopped
1 tbsp all-purpose flour
1/4 cup milk
salt
pinch of cayenne pepper

1 To make the filling, melt the butter in a skillet. Add the celery, garlic, and onion and sauté gently for about 5 minutes, or until softened.

2 Reduce the heat and stir in the flour, then the milk. Bring back to a simmer, then heat gently until the mixture is thick, stirring frequently.

3 Season with salt and cayenne pepper. Let cool.

4 To make the pastry, sift together the flour and salt into a mixing bowl and rub in the butter with your fingertips until well combined. Stir the cheese into the mixture, together with the cold water, and mix to form a dough.

5 Roll out three-quarters of the dough on a lightly floured surface. Using a 2½-inch cookie cutter, cut out 12 rounds. Line a muffin pan with the rounds.

6 Divide the filling between the pie dough rounds. Roll out the remaining dough and, using a 2-inch cutter, cut out 12 rounds. Place the smaller rounds on top of the pie filling and seal well. Make a slit in each pie and chill for 30 minutes.

7 Bake in a preheated oven at 425°F for 15–20 minutes. Cool in the pan for about 10 minutes before turning out. Serve warm.

Asparagus & Goat Cheese Tart

Fresh asparagus is now readily available all year round,
so you can make this tasty supper dish at any time.

Serves 6

INGREDIENTS

9 ounces fresh ready-made
  pie dough

9 ounces asparagus

1 tbsp vegetable oil

1 red onion, finely chopped

$^1/_4$ cup chopped hazelnuts

7 ounces goat cheese

2 eggs, beaten

4 tbsp light cream

salt and pepper

1 On a lightly floured surface, roll out the pie dough and line a 10-inch loose-bottomed quiche pan. Prick the base of the pie dough with a fork and chill in the refrigerator for about 30 minutes.

2 Line the pie shell with foil and dried beans and bake in a preheated oven at 375°F for about 15 minutes.

3 Remove the foil and beans from the pie shell, return to the oven and cook it for a further 15 minutes.

4 Cook the asparagus in boiling water for 2–3 minutes, drain, and cut into bite-size pieces.

5 Heat the oil in a small skillet and sauté the onion until soft and lightly golden in color. Spoon the asparagus, onion, and chopped hazelnuts into the prepared pie shell.

6 Beat together the cheese, eggs, and cream until smooth, or process in a blender until smooth. Season well with salt and pepper, then pour the mixture over the asparagus, onion, and hazelnuts.

7 Bake in the oven for 15–20 minutes, or until the cheese filling is just set. Serve warm or cold.

VARIATION

Omit the hazelnuts and sprinkle Parmesan cheese over the top of the tart just before cooking in the oven, if you prefer.

Onion Tart

This crisp pie shell is filled with onions and cheese and baked until it melts in the mouth.

Serves 6

INGREDIENTS

9 ounces fresh ready-made
   shortcrust pie dough
3 tbsp butter
1/2 cup diced bacon

1 pound 9 ounces onions, peeled and
   sliced thinly
2 eggs, beaten
2/3 cup grated Parmesan cheese

1 tsp dried sage
salt and pepper

1 Roll out the pie dough on a lightly floured counter and line a 10-inch loose-bottomed quiche pan.

2 Prick the base of the pie dough with a fork and chill for 30 minutes.

3 Heat the butter in a saucepan, add the diced bacon and sliced onions, and sweat them over a low heat for about 25 minutes, until tender. If the onion slices start to turn brown, add 1 tablespoon of water to the saucepan.

4 Add the beaten eggs to the onion mixture and stir in the cheese, sage, and salt and pepper to taste.

5 Carefully spoon the onion mixture into the prepared pie shell.

6 Bake in a preheated oven at 350°F for 20–30 minutes, or until the tart has just set.

7 Cool slightly in the pan, then serve the onion tart warm or cold.

VARIATION

For a vegetarian version, replace the bacon with the same quantity of chopped mushrooms.

Pissaladière

This is a variation of the classic Italian pizza, but is made with ready-made puff pie dough. It is perfect for outdoor eating.

Serves 8

INGREDIENTS

4 tbsp olive oil
1 pound 9 ounces red onions,
    thinly sliced
2 garlic cloves, crushed
2 tsp superfine sugar

2 tbsp red wine vinegar
12 ounces fresh ready-made puff
    pastry
salt and pepper

TOPPING:
2 x 1¾ ounce cans anchovy fillets
12 pitted green olives
1 tsp dried marjoram

1 Lightly grease a jelly roll pan. Heat the olive oil in a large saucepan. Add the onions and garlic and cook over a very low heat for about 30 minutes, stirring occasionally.

2 Add the sugar and vinegar to the pan and season with plenty of salt and pepper.

3 On a lightly floured surface, roll out the pastry dough to a rectangle about 13 x 9 inches. Place the dough rectangle onto the prepared jelly roll pan,

pushing the dough well into the corners of the pan.

4 Spread the onion mixture over the dough.

5 Arrange the anchovy fillets and green olives on top, then sprinkle with the marjoram.

6 Bake in a preheated oven at 425°F for approximately 20–25 minutes, until the pissaladière is a light golden color. Serve piping hot, straight from the oven.

VARIATION

Cut the pissaladière into squares or triangles for easy finger food at a party or barbecue.

Mini Cheese & Onion Tarts

Serve these delicious little savory tarts as finger food
at buffets or cocktail parties.

Serves 12

INGREDIENTS

PIE DOUGH:
1 cup all-purpose flour
$1/4$ tsp salt
$1/3$ cup butter, cut into small pieces
1–2 tbsp water

FILLING:
1 egg, beaten
generous $1/3$ cup light cream
$1/2$ cup grated Red Leicester cheese,

3 scallions, finely chopped
salt
cayenne pepper

1 To make the pie dough, sift the flour and salt into a mixing bowl. Rub in the butter with your fingers until well combined and the mixture resembles breadcrumbs. Stir in the water and mix to form a smooth dough.

2 Roll out the pie dough on a lightly floured surface. Using a 3-inch cookie cutter, stamp out 12 rounds from the pie dough and line a muffin pan.

3 To make the filling, whisk together the beaten egg, light cream, grated cheese, and chopped scallions. Season with salt and cayenne.

4 Pour the filling mixture into the pie shells and bake in a preheated oven at 350°F for about 20–25 minutes, or until the filling is just set.

5 Serve the mini tarts warm or cold.

VARIATION

Top each mini tart with slices of fresh tomato before baking, if you prefer.

COOK'S TIP

If you use 6 ounces of ready-made pie dough instead of making it yourself, these tarts can be made in minutes.

Ham & Cheese Lattice Pies

These pretty lattice pies are equally delicious served hot or cold.
They make a good picnic food served with salad.

Makes 6

INGREDIENTS

9 ounces fresh ready-made puff
   pastry
$^1/_3$ cup finely chopped ham

$^2/_3$ cup full-fat soft cheese
2 tbsp chopped fresh chives
1 egg, beaten

2 tbsp freshly grated Parmesan
   cheese
pepper

1 Roll out the pastry thinly on a lightly floured counter. Cut out 12 rectangles measuring 6 x 2 inches.

2 Place the rectangles onto greased cookie sheets and leave to chill in the refrigerator for 30 minutes.

3 Meanwhile, combine the ham, cheese, and chives in a small bowl. Season with pepper to taste.

4 Spread the ham and cheese mixture along the center of 6 of the rectangles, leaving a

1-inch border around each one. Brush the border with a little beaten egg.

5 To make the lattice pattern, fold the remaining rectangles lengthwise. Leaving a 1-inch border, cut vertical lines across one edge of the rectangles using a sharp knife.

6 Unfold the rectangles and place them over the rectangles topped with the ham and cheese mixture set on the cookie sheets. Seal the dough edges well and lightly sprinkle with the grated Parmesan cheese.

7 Bake in a preheated oven at 350°F for 15–20 minutes. Serve hot or cold.

COOK'S TIP

These pies can be made in advance, frozen uncooked, and baked fresh when required.

Vegetarian Baking

Vegetarian food is not a poor substitute for non-meat eaters, it is delicious and nutritious in its own right. The variety of recipes in this chapter will allow vegetarians and vegans to enjoy baking recipes and perhaps to experiment with the fillings and toppings to suit their individuals needs. Some of the recipes include variations of family classics, such as Pineapple Upside-down Cake, Fruit Crumble, and Date & Apricot Tart.

Most supermarkets and health food stores stock a variety of products which are good for vegetarians and it is worth experimenting with several varieties until you find the one you prefer. Useful products include soy milk, which is sold in concentrated form that needs diluting, ready-to-drink form, or in powdered form; and cooking fats, including various brands of vegan margarine and numerous white vegetable fats which are ideal for pastries and frying.

Bean curd is a versatile, whitish, curd-like product, high in protein and cholesterol-free, which can be used in sweet and savory dishes.

Eggless sponges and toppings such as the ones in this chapter are made by adding extra liquid (usually oil) to the mixture and increasing the amount of rising agent.

Curry Turnovers

These turnovers, which are suitable for vegans, are a delicious combination of vegetables and spices. They can be eaten either hot or cold.

Serves 4

INGREDIENTS

1³/₄ cups plain whole-wheat flour
¹/₃ cup vegan margarine, cut into
   small pieces
4 tbsp water
2 tbsp oil

1¹/₄ cups diced root vegetables
   (potatoes, carrots, and parsnips)
1 small onion, chopped
2 garlic cloves, finely chopped
¹/₂ tsp curry powder
¹/₂ tsp ground turmeric

¹/₂ tsp ground cumin
¹/₂ tsp wholegrain mustard
5 tbsp stock
soy milk, to glaze

1 Place the flour in a mixing bowl and rub in the vegan margarine with your fingertips until the mixture resembles breadcrumbs. Stir in the water and bring together to form a soft dough. Wrap and chill in the refrigerator for 30 minutes.

2 To make the filling, heat the oil in a large saucepan. Add the diced root vegetables, chopped onion, and garlic. Sauté for 2 minutes, then stir in all of the spices, turning the vegetables to coat them with the spices. Cook for a further 1 minute.

3 Add the stock to the pan and bring to a boil. Cover and simmer for about 20 minutes, stirring occasionally, until the vegetables are tender and the liquid has been absorbed. Let cool.

4 Divide the pie dough into 4 portions. Roll each portion into a 6-inch round. Place the filling equally on one half of each round.

5 Brush the edges of each round with soy milk, then fold over and press the edges together to seal. Place on a cookie sheet. Bake in a preheated oven at 400°F for 25-30 minutes, until the pastry is a light golden brown color.

COOK'S TIP

The vegetable filling can be made in advance and stored in the refrigerator until required.

Brazil Nut & Mushroom Pie

The button mushrooms give this wholesome vegan pie a wonderful aromatic flavor. The pie can be frozen uncooked and baked from frozen.

Serves 4–6

INGREDIENTS

PIE DOUGH:
1³/4 cups plain whole-wheat flour
¹/3 cup vegan margarine, cut into
   small pieces
4 tbsp water
soy milk, to glaze

FILLING:
2 tbsp vegan margarine
1 onion, chopped
1 garlic clove, finely chopped
2 cups sliced button mushrooms
1 tbsp all-purpose flour
²/3 cup vegetable stock
1 tbsp tomato paste

1¹/2 cups chopped Brazil nuts
1¹/3 cups fresh whole-wheat
   breadcrumbs
2 tbsp chopped fresh parsley
¹/2 tsp pepper

1 To make the pie dough, place the flour in a mixing bowl and rub in the vegan margarine with your fingertips until the mixture resembles fine breadcrumbs. Stir in the water and bring together to form a dough. Wrap and chill for 30 minutes.

2 To make the filling, melt half of the margarine in a skillet. Add the onion, garlic, and mushrooms and sauté for 5 minutes, until softened. Add the flour and cook for 1 minute, stirring frequently. Gradually add the stock, stirring until the sauce is smooth and beginning to thicken. Stir in the tomato paste, Brazil nuts, breadcrumbs, parsley, and pepper. Cool slightly.

3 On a lightly floured surface, roll out two-thirds of the pie dough and use to line an 8-inch loose-bottomed quiche pan or pie dish. Spread the filling in the pie shell. Brush the edges of the pie dough with soy milk. Roll out the remaining pie dough to fit the top of the pie. Seal the edges, make a slit in the top of the pie dough, and brush with soy milk.

4 Bake in a preheated oven at 400°F for 30–40 minutes, until golden brown.

Lentil & Red Bell Pepper Flan

This savory flan combines lentils and red bell peppers in a tasty whole-wheat pie shell. This flan is suitable for vegans.

Serves 6–8

INGREDIENTS

PIE DOUGH:
$1^3/4$ cups plain whole-wheat flour
$1/3$ cup vegan margarine, cut into small pieces
4 tbsp water

FILLING:
$3/4$ cup red lentils, rinsed
$1^1/4$ cups vegetable stock
1 tbsp vegan margarine
1 onion, chopped

2 red bell peppers, cored, seeded, and diced
1 tsp yeast extract
1 tbsp tomato paste
3 tbsp chopped fresh parsley
pepper

1 To make the pie dough, place the flour in a mixing bowl and rub in the vegan margarine with your fingertips until the mixture resembles fine breadcrumbs. Stir in the water and bring together to form a dough. Wrap and chill for 30 minutes.

2 Meanwhile, make the filling. Put the lentils in a saucepan with the stock, bring to a boil, and then simmer for 10 minutes, until the lentils are tender and can be mashed to a purée.

3 Melt the margarine in a small pan, add the chopped onion and diced red bell peppers and sauté until just soft.

4 Add the lentil purée, yeast extract, tomato paste, and parsley. Season with pepper. Mix until well combined.

5 On a lightly floured kitchen counter, roll out the dough and line a 10-inch loose-bottomed quiche pan. Prick the base of the pie dough with a fork and spoon

the lentil purée mixture into the pie shell.

6 Bake in a preheated oven at 400°F for 30 minutes, until the filling is firm.

VARIATION

Add corn to the flan in step 4 for a colorful and tasty change, if you prefer.

Garlic & Sage Bread

*This freshly made bread is an ideal accompaniment
to salads and is suitable for vegans.*

Serves 4–6

INGREDIENTS

$2^{1}/_{4}$ cups strong brown bread flour
1 sachet active dry yeast

3 tbsp chopped fresh sage
2 tsp sea salt
3 garlic cloves, finely chopped

1 tsp honey
$^{2}/_{3}$ cup lukewarm water

1 Grease a cookie sheet. Sift the flour into a large mixing bowl and stir in the husks remaining in the strainer.

2 Stir in the yeast, sage, and half of the sea salt. Reserve 1 teaspoon of the chopped garlic for sprinkling and stir the rest into the bowl. Add the honey with the water and mix together to form a dough.

3 Turn the dough out onto a lightly floured surface and knead it for about 5 minutes (alternatively, use an electric mixer with a dough hook).

4 Place the dough in a greased bowl, cover, and let rise in a warm place until it has doubled in size.

5 Knead the dough again for a few minutes, shape it into a round (see Cook's Tip) and place on the cookie sheet.

6 Cover and let rise for a further 30 minutes, or until springy to the touch. Sprinkle with the rest of the sea salt and garlic.

7 Bake in a preheated oven at 400°F for 25–30 minutes. Cool on a wire rack before serving.

COOK'S TIP

*Roll the dough into a long
sausage and then curve it into
a circular shape.*

VARIATION

*Omit the sea salt for sprinkling over
the top of the bread, if preferred.*

Apricot Slices

These vegan slices are ideal for children's school lunches.
They are full of flavor and made with healthy ingredients.

Makes 12

INGREDIENTS

PIE DOUGH:
1³/₄ cups whole-wheat flour
¹/₂ cup finely ground mixed nuts
¹/₃ cup vegan margarine, cut into
    small pieces
4 tbsp water
soy milk, to glaze

FILLING:
2 cups dried apricots
grated rind of 1 orange
1¹/₃ cups apple juice
1 tsp ground cinnamon
¹/₃ cup raisins

1 Lightly grease a 9-inch square cake pan. To make the pie dough, place the flour and nuts in a mixing bowl and rub in the margarine with your fingers until the mixture resembles breadcrumbs. Stir in the water and bring together to form a dough. Wrap and chill for 30 minutes.

2 To make the filling, place the apricots, orange rind, and apple juice in a saucepan and bring to a boil. Simmer for 30 minutes, until the apricots are mushy. Cool slightly, then blend to a purée. Stir in the ground cinnamon and raisins.

3 Divide the pie dough in half, roll out one half, and use to line the base of the pan. Spread the apricot purée over the top and brush the edges of the pie dough with water. Roll out the rest of the dough to fit over the top of the apricot purée. Press down and seal the edges.

4 Prick the top of the pie dough with a fork and brush with a little soy milk. Bake in a preheated oven at 400°F for 20–25 minutes, until the pastry is a golden color. Cool slightly before cutting into 12 bars. Serve warm or cold.

COOK'S TIP

These slices will keep in an airtight container for 3–4 days.

Baked Bean Curd Cheesecake

This cheesecake has a rich creamy texture, but contains no dairy products. Check the ingredients list on the graham crackers to make sure you buy a brand that is suitable for vegetarians.

Serves 6

INGREDIENTS

2^1/$_2$ cups crushed graham crackers
4 tbsp vegan margarine, melted
^{1}/$_4$ cups pitted, chopped dates

4 tbsp lemon juice
rind of 1 lemon
3 tbsp water
12 ounces firm bean curd

^{2}/$_3$ cup apple juice
1 banana, mashed
1 tsp vanilla extract
1 mango, peeled and chopped

1 Lightly grease a 7-inch round loose-bottomed cake pan with a little butter.

2 Mix together the graham cracker crumbs and melted margarine in a bowl. Press the mixture into the base of the prepared pan.

3 Put the chopped dates, lemon juice, lemon rind, and water into a saucepan and bring to a boil. Simmer for 5 minutes until the dates are soft, then mash them roughly with a fork.

4 Place the mixture in a blender or food processor with the bean curd, apple juice, mashed banana, and vanilla extract and process until the mixture is a thick, smooth purée.

5 Pour the bean curd purée into the prepared graham cracker crumb base.

6 Bake in a preheated oven at 350°F for 30–40 minutes, until lightly golden in color. Cool in the pan, then chill thoroughly before serving.

7 Place the chopped mango in a blender and process until smooth. Serve it as a sauce with the chilled cheesecake.

VARIATION

Silken bean curd may be substituted for the firm bean curd to give a softer texture; it will take 40–50 minutes to set.

Pineapple Upside-down Cake

This upside-down cake shows how a classic favorite can be adapted for vegans by making the cake with vegan margarine and oil instead of butter and eggs.

Serves 6

INGREDIENTS

15 ounce can unsweetened pineapple pieces, drained and juice reserved

4 tsp cornstarch

3 tbsp light brown sugar

4 tbsp vegan margarine, cut into small pieces

$\frac{1}{2}$ cup water

rind of 1 lemon

SPONGE:

$\frac{1}{4}$ cup sunflower oil

$\frac{1}{3}$ cup light brown sugar

$\frac{2}{3}$ cup water

$1\frac{1}{4}$ cups all-purpose flour

2 tsp baking powder

1 tsp ground cinnamon

1 Grease a deep 7-inch cake pan. Mix the reserved juice from the pineapple with the cornstarch until it forms a smooth paste. Put the paste in a saucepan with the sugar, vegan margarine, and water and stir over a low heat until the sugar has dissolved. Bring to a boil and simmer for 2–3 minutes, until thickened. Cool slightly.

2 To make the sponge, place the oil, sugar, and water in a saucepan. Heat gently until the sugar has dissolved; do not allow it to boil. Remove from the heat and cool. Sift the flour, baking powder, and ground cinnamon into a mixing bowl. Add the cooled sugar syrup and beat well to form a batter.

3 Place the pineapple pieces and lemon rind on the bottom of the pan and pour 4 tbsp of the pineapple syrup over the pineapple. Spoon the sponge batter on top.

4 Bake in a preheated oven at 350°F for 35–40 minutes, until set and a knife inserted into the center comes out clean. Invert onto a plate, let stand for 5 minutes, then remove the pan. Serve the cake with the remaining syrup.

VARIATION

Add $\frac{1}{4}$ cup golden raisins to the pineapple pieces, if you prefer.

Date & Apricot Tart

*There is no need to add any extra sugar to this filling because the
dried fruit is naturally sweet. This tart is suitable for vegans.*

Serves 6–8

INGREDIENTS

1³/₄ cups plain whole-wheat flour
¹/₂ cup ground mixed nuts
¹/₃ cup vegan margarine, cut into
small pieces

4 tbsp water
2 cups dried apricots, chopped
1¹/₃ cups pitted, chopped dates
2 cups apple juice

1 tsp ground cinnamon
grated rind of 1 lemon
soy custard, to serve (optional)

1 Place the flour and ground nuts in a mixing bowl and rub in the margarine with your fingertips until the mixture resembles breadcrumbs. Stir in the water and bring together to form a dough. Wrap the dough and chill for 30 minutes.

2 Meanwhile, place the apricots and dates in a saucepan with the apple juice, cinnamon, and lemon rind. Bring to a boil, cover, and simmer for 15 minutes, until the fruit softens and can be mashed to a purée.

3 Reserve a small ball of pie dough for making lattice strips. On a lightly floured surface, roll out the rest of the dough to form a round and use to line a 9-inch loose-bottomed quiche pan.

4 Spread the fruit filling over the base of the pie dough. Roll out the reserved pie dough and cut into strips ¹/₂ inch wide. Cut the strips to fit the tart and twist them across the top of the fruit to form a lattice pattern. Moisten the edges of the strips with water and seal to the rim.

5 Bake in a preheated oven at 400°F for 25–30 minutes, until golden brown. Cut into slices and serve with soy custard, if using.

Fruit Crumble

Any fruits in season can be used in this wholesome pudding.
It is suitable for vegans as it contains no dairy products.

Serves 6

INGREDIENTS

6 eating pears, peeled, cored,
   quartered, and sliced
1 tbsp chopped preserved ginger
1 tbsp molasses
2 tbsp orange juice

TOPPING:
$1^1/_2$ cups all-purpose flour
$^1/_3$ cup vegan margarine, cut into
   small pieces
$^1/_4$ cup slivered almonds
$^1/_3$ cup dried oats
$^1/_8$ cup molasses

soy custard, to serve

1 Lightly grease a 5 cup ovenproof dish.

2 In a bowl, mix together the pears, ginger, molasses, and orange juice. Spoon the mixture into the prepared dish.

3 To make the crumble topping, sift the flour into a mixing bowl and rub in the margarine with your fingers until well combined and the mixture resembles fine breadcrumbs. Stir in the slivered almonds, oats, and molasses. Mix together until all the ingredients are well combined.

4 Sprinkle the crumble topping evenly over the pear and ginger mixture in the dish.

5 Bake in a preheated oven at 375°F for 30 minutes, until the topping is golden and the fruit is tender. Serve with soy custard, if using.

VARIATION

Stir 1 tsp apple pie spice into the crumble mixture in step 3 for added flavor, if you prefer.

Eggless Sponge Cake

*This is a healthy variation of the classic Victoria sponge
layer cake and is suitable for vegans.*

Makes one 8-inch cake

INGREDIENTS

1³/₄ cups self-rising whole-
wheat flour
2 tsp baking powder

³/₄ cup superfine sugar
6 tbsp sunflower oil
1 cup water

1 tsp vanilla extract
4 tbsp strawberry or raspberry
reduced-sugar spread
superfine sugar, for dusting

1 Thoroughly grease two
8-inch layer pans with butter
and line them with baking
parchment.

2 Sift the flour and baking
powder into a large mixing
bowl, stirring in any bran
remaining in the strainer. Stir in
the superfine sugar.

3 Pour in the sunflower oil,
water, and vanilla extract and
mix together with a wooden
spoon for about 1 minute until the
cake mixture is a smooth
consistency.

4 Divide the mixture between
the prepared pans.

5 Bake in a preheated oven at
350°F for approximately
25–30 minutes, until the center
springs back when lightly touched.
Cool in the pans before turning
out and transferring to a wire rack.

6 To serve, remove the baking
parchment and place one of
the sponges onto a serving plate.
Cover with the strawberry or
raspberry spread and place the
other sponge on top. Dust with a
little superfine sugar.

VARIATION

*Use melted vegan butter or
margarine instead of the
sunflower oil if you prefer, but
allow it to cool before adding it
to the dry ingredients in step 3.*

Cakes

This chapter includes a variety of different cakes, depending on the time you have and the effort you want to spend. Small cakes include Gingerbread, Carrot Squares, and White Chocolate & Apricot Squares. These cakes are easier to prepare and cook than larger ones and, in general, are particular favorites to have with a cup of coffee or to provide for a child's school lunch.

Cakes such as Almond Cake and Lemon Syrup Cake are made very quickly using baking powder, which produces quick, well-risen cakes.

Others require special ingredients to produce cakes with that "'little something extra." Look for the Olive Oil, Fruit, & Nut Cake, Candied Fruit Cake, and Coffee & Almond Streusel Cake. This chapter also includes a selection of scones and muffins.

Olive Oil, Fruit, & Nut Cake

It is well worth using a good quality olive oil for this cake, as this will determine its flavor. The cake will keep well in an airtight container until ready to eat.

Serves 8

INGREDIENTS

2 cups self-rising flour
4 tbsp superfine sugar

$^1/_2$ cup milk
4 tbsp orange juice
$^2/_3$ cup olive oil

$^2/_3$ cup mixed dried fruit
$^1/_4$ cup pine nuts

1 Grease a 7-inch cake pan with a little butter and line with baking parchment.

2 Sift the flour into a large mixing bowl and stir in the superfine sugar.

3 Make a well in the center of the dry ingredients and pour in the milk and orange juice. Stir the mixture with a wooden spoon, beating in the flour and sugar.

4 Pour in the olive oil, stirring well so that all of the ingredients are evenly mixed.

5 Stir the mixed dried fruit and pine nuts into the mixture and spoon into the prepared pan.

6 Bake in a preheated oven at 350°F for about 45 minutes, until the cake is golden and firm to the touch.

7 Leave the cake to cool in the pan for a few minutes before transferring to a wire rack to cool further.

8 Serve the cake warm or cold and cut into slices.

COOK'S TIP

Pine nuts are best known as the flavoring ingredient in the classic Italian pesto, but here they give a delicate, slightly resinous flavor to this cake.

Chocolate & Pear Sponge Cake

*What could be better than the lovely combination used in this cake
of chocolate and fresh pears in a moist sponge.*

Serves 6

INGREDIENTS

^{3}/4 cup butter, softened
1 cup light brown sugar
3 eggs, beaten

1^1/4 cups self-rising flour
2 tbsp unsweetened cocoa

2 tbsp milk
2 small pears, peel, cored, and sliced

1 Thoroughly grease an 8-inch loose-bottomed cake pan and line the base with baking parchment.

2 In a bowl, cream together the butter and brown sugar until pale and fluffy.

3 Gradually add the beaten eggs to the creamed mixture, beating well after each addition.

4 Sift the self-rising flour and unsweetened cocoa into the creamed mixture and fold in gently until all of the ingredients are combined.

5 Stir in the milk until well combined, then spoon the mixture into the prepared pan. Level the surface with the back of a spoon or a knife.

6 Place the pear slices on top of the cake mixture, arranging them in a radiating pattern.

7 Bake in a preheated oven at 350°F for about 1 hour, until the cake is just firm to the touch.

8 Let the cake cool in the pan, then transfer to a wire rack until completely cold before serving.

COOK'S TIP

Serve the cake with melted chocolate drizzled over the top for a delicious dessert.

Caraway Madeira

This is a classic Madeira cake made in the traditional way with caraway seeds. If you do not like their flavor, they can be omitted.

Serves 8

INGREDIENTS

1 cup butter, softened
1 cup light brown sugar
3 eggs, beaten

3 cups self-rising flour
1 tbsp caraway seeds

grated rind of 1 lemon
6 tbsp milk
1 or 2 strips of citron peel

1 Grease and line a 2 pound loaf pan.

2 In a bowl, cream together the butter and brown sugar until pale and fluffy.

3 Gradually add the beaten eggs to the creamed mixture, beating well after each addition.

4 Sift the flour into the bowl and gently fold into the creamed mixture.

5 Add the caraway seeds, lemon rind, and the milk and fold in until thoroughly blended.

6 Spoon the mixture into the prepared pan and level the surface with a knife.

7 Bake in a preheated oven at 325°F for 20 minutes.

8 Remove the cake from the oven, place the pieces of citron peel on top of the cake, and return it to the oven for a further 40 minutes, or until the cake is well risen and a knife inserted into the center comes out clean.

9 Let the cake cool in the pan before turning out and

transferring to a wire rack until completely cold.

COOK'S TIP

Citron peel is available in the baking section of supermarkets. If it is unavailable, you can substitute it with chopped candied peel.

Clementine Cake

This cake is flavored with clementine rind and juice, creating a rich buttery cake, but one full of fresh fruit flavor.

Serves 8

INGREDIENTS

2 clementines
3/4 cup butter, softened
3/4 cup superfine sugar
3 eggs, beaten

1 1/2 cups self-rising flour
3 tbsp ground almonds
3 tbsp light cream

GLAZE AND TOPPING:
6 tbsp clementine juice
2 tbsp superfine sugar
3 white sugar cubes, crushed

1 Thoroughly grease a 7-inch round pan and line the base with baking parchment.

2 Pare the rind from the clementines and chop the rind finely. In a bowl, cream together the butter, sugar, and clementine rind until pale and fluffy.

3 Gradually add the beaten eggs to the mixture, beating well after each addition.

4 Gently fold in the self-rising flour, followed by the ground almonds, and the light cream. Spoon the mixture into the prepared pan.

5 Bake in a preheated oven at 350°F for approximately 55–60 minutes, or until a knife inserted into the center of the cake comes out clean. Cool slightly.

6 Meanwhile, make the glaze. Put the clementine juice into a small saucepan with the superfine sugar. Bring to a boil and simmer for 5 minutes.

7 Drizzle the glaze over the cake until it has been absorbed, and sprinkle with the crushed sugar cubes.

COOK'S TIP

If you prefer, chop the rind from the clementines in a food processor or blender together with the sugar in step 2. Tip the mixture into a bowl with the butter and begin to cream the mixture.

Candied Fruit Cake

This cake is extremely colorful; you can choose any mixture of candied fruits or stick to just one type if you prefer.

Serves 8

INGREDIENTS

3/4 cup butter, softened
3/4 cup superfine sugar
3 eggs, beaten

1 1/2 cups self-rising flour, sifted
3 tbsp ground rice
finely grated rind of 1 lemon

4 tbsp lemon juice
2/3 cup candied fruits, chopped
confectioners' sugar, for dusting (optional)

1 Lightly grease a 7-inch cake pan and line with baking parchment.

2 In a bowl, whisk together the butter and superfine sugar until light and fluffy.

3 Add the beaten eggs, a little at a time. Using a metal spoon, fold in the flour and ground rice.

4 Add the grated lemon rind and juice, followed by the chopped candied fruits. Lightly mix all the ingredients together.

5 Spoon the mixture into the prepared pan and level the surface with the back of a spoon or a knife.

6 Bake in a preheated oven at 350°F for 1–1 hour 10 minutes, until well risen or until a knife inserted into the center of the cake comes out clean.

7 Let the cake cool in the pan for 5 minutes, then turn out onto a wire rack and cool completely.

8 Dust well with a little confectioners' sugar, if using, before serving.

COOK'S TIP

Wash and dry the candied fruits before chopping them. This will prevent the fruits sinking to the bottom of the cake during cooking.

White Chocolate & Apricot Squares

The white chocolate makes this a very rich cake, so serve it cut into small bars or squares, or sliced thinly.

Makes 12 bars

INGREDIENTS

$^1/_2$ cup butter
6 ounces white chocolate, chopped
4 eggs

$^1/_2$ cup superfine sugar
$1^3/_4$ cups all-purpose flour, sifted

1 tsp baking powder
pinch of salt
$^1/_2$ cup chopped ready-to-eat dried apricots

1 Lightly grease a 9-inch square cake pan with a little butter or margarine and line the base of the pan with a sheet of baking parchment.

2 Melt the butter and chocolate in a double boiler. Stir frequently with a wooden spoon until the mixture is smooth and glossy. Let the mixture cool slightly.

3 Beat the eggs and superfine sugar into the butter and chocolate mixture until well combined.

4 Fold in the flour, baking powder, salt, and chopped dried apricots and mix well.

5 Pour the mixture into the prepared pan and bake in a preheated oven at 350°F for 25–30 minutes.

6 The center of the cake may not be completely firm, but it will set as it cools. Leave in the pan to cool.

7 When the cake is completely cold turn it out and slice into bars or squares.

VARIATION

Replace the white chocolate with milk or dark chocolate, if you prefer.

Crunchy Fruit Cake

The cornmeal adds texture to this fruit cake, as well as an interesting golden yellow color. It also acts as a flour, binding the ingredients together to create a lighter texture.

Serves 8–10

INGREDIENTS

$^1/_3$ cup butter, softened
$^1/_2$ cup superfine sugar
2 eggs, beaten

$^1/_3$ cup self-rising flour, sifted
$^2/_3$ cup cornmeal
1 tsp baking powder

$1^2/_3$ cups mixed dried fruit
$^1/_4$ cup pine nuts
grated rind of 1 lemon
4 tbsp lemon juice
2 tbsp milk

1 Thoroughly grease a 7-inch cake pan and line the base with baking parchment.

2 In a bowl, whisk together the butter and sugar until light and fluffy.

3 Whisk in the beaten eggs, a little at a time, whisking well after each addition.

4 Gently fold the sifted flour, baking powder, and cornmeal into the mixture until thoroughly blended.

5 Stir in the mixed dried fruit, pine nuts, grated lemon rind, lemon juice, and milk.

6 Spoon the mixture into the prepared pan and level the surface with a knife.

7 Bake in a preheated oven at 350°F for about 1 hour, or until a knife inserted into the center of the cake comes out clean.

8 Leave the cake to cool in the pan before turning out.

VARIATION

To give a more crumbly light fruit cake, omit the cornmeal and use $1^1/_4$ cups self-rising flour instead.

Chocolate Slab Cake with Frosting

This chocolate slab cake gets its moist texture from the sour cream which is stirred into the beaten mixture.

Serves 10–12

INGREDIENTS

1 cup butter
3 1/2 ounces dark chocolate, chopped
2/3 cup water
2 1/2 cups all-purpose flour
2 tsp baking powder

1 2/3 cups light brown sugar
2/3 cup sour cream
2 eggs, beaten

FROSTING:
7 ounces dark chocolate
6 tbsp water
3 tbsp light cream
1 tbsp butter, chilled

1 Thoroughly grease a 13 x 8-inch square cake pan and line the base with baking parchment. In a saucepan, melt the butter and chocolate, together with the water over a low heat, stirring frequently.

2 Sift the flour and baking powder into a mixing bowl and stir in the sugar.

3 Pour the hot chocolate liquid into the bowl and then beat well until all of the ingredients are evenly mixed. Stir in the sour cream, followed by the eggs.

4 Pour the mixture into the prepared pan and bake in a preheated oven at 375°F for 40–45 minutes.

5 Let the cake cool in the pan before turning it out onto a wire rack. Cool completely.

6 To make the frosting, melt the chocolate with the water in a saucepan over a very low heat, stir in the cream, and remove from the heat. Stir in the chilled butter, then pour the frosting over the cooled cake, using a spatula to spread it evenly over the top of the cake.

COOK'S TIP

Leave the cake on the wire rack to frost it and place a large cookie sheet underneath to catch any drips.

Chocolate & Almond Torte

This torte is perfect for serving on a hot sunny day with heavy cream and a selection of fresh summer berries.

Serves 10

INGREDIENTS

8 ounces dark chocolate, broken
    into pieces
3 tbsp water
1 cup light brown sugar
$^3/_4$ cup butter, softened

$^1/_4$ cup ground almonds
3 tbsp self-rising flour
5 eggs, separated
$^1/_4$ cup blanched almonds,
    finely chopped

confectioners' sugar, for dusting
heavy cream, to serve (optional)

1 Grease a 9-inch loose-bottomed cake pan and base line with baking parchment.

2 In a saucepan set over a very low heat, melt the chocolate with the water, stirring until smooth. Add the sugar and stir until dissolved, taking the pan off the heat to prevent it overheating.

3 Add the butter in small amounts until it has melted into the chocolate. Remove from the heat and lightly stir in the ground almonds and flour. Add the egg yolks, one at a time, beating well after each addition.

4 In a large mixing bowl, whisk the egg whites until they stand in soft peaks, then fold them into the chocolate mixture with a metal spoon. Stir in the chopped almonds. Pour the mixture into the pan and level the surface.

5 Bake in a preheated oven at 350°F for 40–45 minutes, until well risen and firm (the cake will crack on the surface during cooking).

6 Let the cake cool in the pan for 30–40 minutes, then turn it out onto a wire rack to cool completely. Dust with the top with confectioners' sugar, cut the cake in slices, and serve with heavy cream, if using.

COOK'S TIP

For a nuttier flavor, toast the chopped almonds in a dry skillet over a medium heat for about 2 minutes, until lightly golden in color.

Carrot Cake

This classic favorite is always popular with children
and adults alike whatever time of day it is served.

Makes 12 bars

INGREDIENTS

1 cup self-rising flour
pinch of salt
1 tsp ground cinnamon
$^3/_4$ cup light brown sugar
2 eggs
scant $^1/_2$ cup sunflower oil
1 cup finely grated carrot
$^1/_3$ cup shredded coconut

$^1/_3$ cup walnuts, chopped
walnut pieces, for decoration

FROSTING:
4 tbsp butter, softened
$^1/_4$ cup full-fat cream cheese
$1^1/_2$ cups confectioners' sugar, sifted
1 tsp lemon juice

1 Lightly grease an 8-inch square cake pan and line with baking parchment.

2 Sift the flour, salt, and ground cinnamon into a large bowl and stir in the brown sugar. Add the eggs and oil to the dry ingredients and mix well.

3 Stir in the grated carrot, shredded coconut, and chopped walnuts.

4 Pour the mixture into the prepared cake pan and bake in a preheated oven at 350°F for 20–25 minutes or until it feels just firm to the touch. Cool in the pan.

5 Meanwhile, make the cheese frosting. In a bowl, beat together the butter, full fat soft cheese, confectioners' sugar, and lemon juice until the mixture is fluffy and creamy.

6 Turn the cake out of the pan and cut into 12 bars or slices. Spread with the frosting and then decorate with walnut pieces.

VARIATION

For a moister cake, replace
the coconut with 1 roughly
mashed banana.

Lemon Syrup Cake

*The lovely light and tangy flavor of the sponge is balanced
by the lemony syrup poured over the top of the cake.*

Serves 8

INGREDIENTS

1³/4 cups all-purpose flour
2 tsp baking powder
1 cup superfine sugar

4 eggs
²/3 cup sour cream
grated rind 1 large lemon
4 tbsp lemon juice
²/3 cup sunflower oil

SYRUP:
4 tbsp confectioners' sugar
3 tbsp lemon juice

1 Lightly grease an 8-inch loose-bottomed round cake pan and line the base with baking parchment.

2 Sift the flour and baking powder into a mixing bowl and stir in the sugar.

3 In a separate bowl, whisk the eggs, sour cream, lemon rind, lemon juice, and oil together.

4 Pour the egg mixture into the dry ingredients and mix well until evenly combined.

5 Pour the mixture into the prepared pan and bake in a preheated oven at 350°F for 45–60 minutes, until risen and golden brown.

6 Meanwhile, to make the syrup, mix together the confectioners' sugar and lemon juice in a small saucepan. Stir over a low heat until just beginning to bubble and turn syrupy.

7 As soon as the cake comes out of the oven prick the surface with a knife, then brush the syrup over the top. Let the cake cool completely in the pan before turning out and serving.

COOK'S TIP

Pricking the surface of the hot cake ensures that the syrup seeps right into the cake and the full flavor is absorbed.

Orange Kugelhopf Cake

Baking in a deep, fluted kugelhopf pan ensures that you create a cake with a stunning shape. The moist cake is full of fresh orange flavor.

Serves 6–8

INGREDIENTS

1 cup butter, softened
1 cup superfine sugar
4 eggs, separated
3 ³/₄ cups all-purpose flour
3 tsp baking powder
pinch of salt

1 ¹/₄ cups fresh orange juice
1 tbsp orange flower water
1 tsp grated orange rind

SYRUP:
³/₄ cup orange juice
1 cup sugar

1 Grease and flour a 10-inch kugelhopf pan or deep ring mold.

2 In a bowl, cream together the butter and superfine sugar until light and fluffy. Add the egg yolks, one at a time, whisking well after each addition.

3 Sift together the flour, salt, and baking powder into a separate bowl. Fold the dry ingredients and the orange juice alternately into the creamed mixture with a metal spoon, working as lightly as possible. Stir in the orange flower water and orange rind.

4 Whisk the egg whites until they reach the soft peak stage and fold them into the mixture.

5 Pour into the prepared mold and bake in a preheated oven at 350°F for 50–55 minutes, or until a knife inserted into center of the cake comes out clean.

6 In a saucepan bring the orange juice and sugar to a boil, then simmer for 5 minutes, until the sugar has dissolved.

7 Remove the cake from the oven and cool in the pan for 10 minutes. Prick the top of the cake with a knife and brush over half of the syrup. Let the cake cool for another 10 minutes. Invert the cake onto a wire rack placed over a deep plate and brush the syrup over the cake until it is entirely covered. Serve.

Coconut Cake

This is a great family favorite. I was always delighted to find it included in my school lunch and considered it a real treat!

Serves 6–8

INGREDIENTS

2 cups self-rising flour
pinch of salt
1/2 cup butter, cut into small pieces

1/2 cup raw crystal sugar
1 cup shredded coconut, plus extra
  for sprinkling

2 eggs, beaten
4 tbsp milk

1 Thoroughly grease a 2-pound loaf pan and line the base with baking parchment.

2 Sift the flour and salt into a mixing bowl and rub in the butter with your fingertips until the mixture resembles fine breadcrumbs.

3 Stir in the sugar, coconut, eggs, and milk and mix to a soft dropping consistency.

4 Spoon the mixture into the prepared pan and level the surface. Bake in a preheated oven at 325°F for 30 minutes.

5 Remove the cake from the oven and sprinkle with the reserved coconut. Return the cake to the oven and cook for a further 30 minutes, until well risen with a light golden brown color, and a knife inserted into the center comes out clean.

6 Let the cake cool in the pan before turning out and transferring to a wire rack to cool completely before serving.

COOK'S TIP

The flavor of this cake is enhanced by storing it in a cool dry place for a few days before eating.

Apple Cake with Cider

This can be eaten as a cake with a cup of coffee, or it can be warmed through and served with cream for a dessert.

Makes an 8-inch cake

INGREDIENTS

2 cups self-rising flour
1 tsp baking powder
$^{1}/_{3}$ cup butter, cut into small pieces

$^{1}/_{3}$ cup superfine sugar
$3^{1}/_{2}$ cups chopped dried apple
5 tbsp raisins

$^{2}/_{3}$ cup sweet cider
1 egg, beaten
1 cup raspberries

1 Thoroughly grease an 8-inch cake pan and line with baking parchment.

2 Sift the flour and baking powder into a mixing bowl and rub in the butter with your fingers until the mixture resembles fine breadcrumbs.

3 Stir in the superfine sugar, chopped dried apple, and the raisins.

4 Pour in the sweet cider and egg and mix together until thoroughly blended. Stir in the raspberries very gently so they do not break up.

5 Pour the mixture into the prepared cake pan.

6 Bake in a preheated oven at 375°F for about 40 minutes, until well risen and a light golden color.

7 Let the cake cool in the pan, then turn out onto a wire rack. Leave until completely cold before serving.

VARIATION

If you don't want to use cider, replace it with clear apple juice, if you prefer.

Spiced Apple Ring

The addition of pieces of fresh apple and crunchy almonds to the cake mixture makes this beautifully moist, yet with a crunch to it.

Serves 8

INGREDIENTS

³/₄ cup butter, softened
³/₄ cup superfine sugar
3 eggs, beaten

1¹/₂ cups self-rising flour
1 tsp ground cinnamon
1 tsp apple pie spice

2 eating apples, cored and grated
2 tbsp apple juice or milk
¹/₄ cup slivered almonds

1 Lightly grease a 10 inch ovenproof ring mold.

2 In a mixing bowl, cream together the butter and sugar until light and fluffy. Gradually add the beaten eggs, beating well after each addition.

3 Sift the flour and spices, then carefully fold them into the creamed mixture.

4 Stir in the grated apples and the apple juice or milk and mix together to form a soft dropping consistency.

5 Sprinkle the slivered almonds around the base of the mold and spoon the cake mixture on top. Level the surface with the back of the spoon.

6 Bake in a preheated oven at 350°F for about 30 minutes, until well risen and a knife inserted into the center comes out clean.

7 Let the cake cool in the pan before turning out and transferring to a wire rack to cool completely. Serve the apple ring cut into slices.

COOK'S TIP

This cake can also be made in a 7-inch round cake pan if you do not have an ovenproof ring mold.

Marbled Chocolate Cake

Separate chocolate and orange cake mixtures are combined in the ring mold to achieve the marbled effect in this light sponge cake.

Serves 8

INGREDIENTS

$^3/_4$ cup butter, softened
$^3/_4$ cup superfine sugar
3 eggs, beaten

1$^1/_4$ cups self-rising flour, sifted
$^1/_4$ cup unsweetened cocoa, sifted

5–6 tbsp orange juice
grated rind of 1 orange

1 Lightly grease a 10-inch ovenproof ring mold.

2 In a mixing bowl, cream together the butter and sugar with an electric mixer for about 5 minutes.

3 Add the beaten egg, a little at a time, beating well after each addition.

4 Using a metal spoon, carefully fold the flour into the creamed mixture. When it has all been incorporated, spoon half of the mixture into a separate mixing bowl.

5 Fold the cocoa and half of the orange juice into one bowl and mix gently.

6 Fold the orange rind and remaining orange juice into the other bowl and mix gently.

7 Place spoonfuls of each of the mixtures alternately into the mold, then drag a knife through the mixture to create a marbled effect.

8 Bake in a preheated oven at 350°F for 30–35 minutes, until well risen and a knife inserted into the center comes out clean.

9 Let the cake cool in the mold before turning out onto a wire rack.

VARIATION

For a richer chocolate flavor, add $^1/_3$ cup chocolate chips to the cocoa mixture.

Coffee & Almond Streusel Cake

*This cake has a moist coffee sponge on the bottom,
covered with a crisp crunchy, spicy topping.*

Serves 8

INGREDIENTS

1¹/₄ cups all-purpose flour
1 tbsp baking powder
¹/₃ cup superfine sugar
²/₃ cup milk
2 eggs
¹/₂ cup butter, melted and cooled
2 tbsp instant coffee mixed with
   1 tbsp boiling water
¹/₃ cup almonds, chopped

confectioners' sugar, for dusting

TOPPING:
¹/₂ cup self-rising flour
¹/₃ cup raw crystal sugar
2 tbsp butter, cut into
   small pieces
1 tsp apple pie spice
1 tbsp water

1 Thoroughly grease a 9-inch loose-bottomed round cake pan and line with baking parchment. Sift together the flour and baking powder into a large mixing bowl, then stir in the superfine sugar.

2 Whisk the milk, eggs, butter, and coffee mixture together and pour onto the dry ingredients. Add the chopped almonds and mix lightly together. Spoon the mixture into the pan.

3 To make the topping, mix the flour and raw crystal sugar together in a separate bowl.

4 Rub in the butter with your fingers until the mixture is crumbly. Sprinkle in the apple pie spice and the water and bring the mixture together in loose crumbs.

Sprinkle the topping over the cake mixture.

5 Bake in a preheated oven at 375°F for 50 minutes–1 hour. Cover loosely with foil if the topping starts to brown too quickly. Let the cake cool in the pan, then turn out to cool completely. Dust with a little confectioners' sugar just before serving.

Sugar-free Fruit Cake

*This cake is full of flavor from the mixed fruits. The fruit gives
the cake its sweetness, so there is no need for extra sugar.*

Serves 8–10

INGREDIENTS

3 cups all-purpose flour
2 tsp baking powder
1 tsp apple pie spice
1/2 cup butter, cut into small pieces
3/4 cup chopped ready-to-eat
  dried apricots

1/2 cup pitted chopped dates
1/2 cup candied cherries, chopped
2/3 cup raisins
1/2 cup milk
2 eggs, beaten
grated rind of 1 orange

5–6 tbsp orange juice
3 tbsp clear honey

1 Grease an 8-inch round cake pan and line the base with baking parchment.

2 Sift the flour, baking powder, and apple pie spice into a large mixing bowl.

3 Rub in the butter with your fingers until the mixture resembles fine breadcrumbs.

4 Carefully stir in the chopped apricots, dates, candied cherries, and raisins with the milk, beaten eggs, grated orange rind, and orange juice and mix together until well combined.

5 Stir in the honey and mix everything together to form a soft dropping consistency. Spoon the mixture into the prepared cake pan and level the surface.

6 Bake in a preheated oven at 350°F for 1 hour until a knife inserted into the center of the cake comes out clean.

7 Let the cake cool in the pan before turning out.

VARIATION

For a fruity alternative, replace the honey with 1 mashed ripe banana, if you prefer.

Almond Cake

*Being glazed with a honey syrup after baking gives this almond-flavored cake
a lovely moist texture, but it can be eaten without the glaze, if preferred.*

Serves 8

INGREDIENTS

¹/₃ cup soft margarine
3 tbsp light brown sugar
2 eggs
1¹/₂ cups self-rising flour
1 tsp baking powder

4 tbsp milk
2 tbsp clear honey
¹/₂ cup slivered almonds

SYRUP:
²/₃ cup clear honey
2 tbsp lemon juice

1 Thoroughly grease a 7-inch round cake pan and line with baking parchment.

2 Place the margarine, brown sugar, eggs, flour, baking powder, milk, and honey in a large mixing bowl and beat well with a wooden spoon for about 1 minute, until all of the ingredients are thoroughly mixed together.

3 Spoon into the prepared pan, level the surface with the back of a spoon or a knife, and sprinkle with the almonds.

4 Bake the mixture in a preheated oven at 350°F for about 50 minutes, or until the cake is well risen.

5 Meanwhile, make the syrup. Combine the honey and lemon juice in a small saucepan and simmer for about 5 minutes, or until the syrup starts to coat the back of a spoon.

6 As soon as the cake comes out of the oven, pour the syrup on top, allowing it to seep into the middle of the cake.

7 Let the cake cool for at least 2 hours before slicing.

COOK'S TIP

Experiment with different flavored honeys for the syrup glaze until you find one that you think tastes best.

Gingerbread

*This spicy gingerbread is made even more moist
by the addition of chopped fresh apples.*

Makes 12 bars

INGREDIENTS

²/₃ cup butter
1 cup light brown sugar
2 tbsp molasses
2 cups all-purpose flour

1 tsp baking powder
2 tsp baking soda
2 tsp ground ginger
²/₃ cup milk

1 egg, beaten
2 eating apples, peeled, chopped, and
   coated with 1 tbsp lemon juice

1 Thoroughly grease a 9-inch square cake pan and line with baking parchment.

2 Melt the butter, sugar, and molasses in a saucepan over a low heat and let the mixture cool.

3 Sift the flour, baking powder, soda, and ginger into a mixing bowl.

4 Stir in the milk, beaten egg, and cooled butter, sugar, and molasses mixture, followed by the chopped apples coated with the lemon juice.

5 Mix everything together gently, then pour the mixture into the prepared pan.

6 Bake in a preheated oven at 325°F for 30–35 minutes, until the cake has risen and a knife inserted into the center comes out clean.

7 Let the cake cool in the pan before turning out and cutting into 12 bars.

VARIATION

*If you enjoy the flavor of ginger, try adding 2 tablespoons finely chopped preserved ginger
to the mixture in step 3.*

Apple Shortcakes

This traditional American dessert is a freshly baked sweet scone, split and filled with sliced apples and whipped cream. The shortcakes can be eaten warm or cold.

Serves 8

INGREDIENTS

1¼ cups all-purpose flour
½ tsp salt
1 tsp baking powder
1 tbsp superfine sugar
1 tbsp butter, cut into
    small pieces
¼ cup milk

confectioners' sugar, for dusting

FILLING:
3 eating apples, peeled, cored,
    and sliced
½ cup superfine sugar
1 tbsp lemon juice

1 tsp ground cinnamon
1⅓ cups water
⅔ cup heavy cream, whipped lightly

1 Lightly grease a cookie sheet.

2 Sift together the flour, salt, and baking powder into a mixing bowl. Stir in the sugar, then rub in the butter with your fingertips until the mixture resembles fine breadcrumbs.

3 Pour in the milk and mix everything to a soft dough. On a lightly floured surface, knead the dough lightly, then roll out to a thickness of ½ inch. Stamp out 4 rounds, using a 2-inch cutter. Transfer the rounds to the prepared cookie sheet.

4 Bake in a preheated oven at 425°F for about 15 minutes, until the shortcakes are well risen and lightly browned. Let cool while you make the filling.

5 To make the filling, place the apple slices, sugar, lemon juice, and cinnamon in a saucepan.

6 Add the water, bring to a boil, and simmer uncovered for 5–10 minutes, until the apples are tender. Cool a little, then remove the apples from the pan.

7 To serve, split the shortcakes in half. Place each bottom half on an individual serving plate and spoon on a quarter of the apple slices, then the cream. Place the other half of the shortcake on top. Serve dusted with confectioners' sugar, if desired.

Rich Scones

*These scones are light and buttery like traditional scones, but they have
a deliciously rich flavor which comes from the molasses.*

Makes 8

INGREDIENTS

2 cups self-rising flour
1 tbsp superfine sugar
pinch of salt

¹/₃ cup butter, cut into small pieces
1 eating apple, peeled, cored,
    and chopped

1 egg, beaten
2 tbsp molasses
5 tbsp milk

1 Lightly grease a cookie sheet with a little butter.

2 Sift the flour, sugar, and salt into a mixing bowl.

3 Rub in the butter with your fingers until the mixture resembles fine breadcrumbs.

4 Stir the chopped apple into the mixture until combined.

5 Mix the beaten egg, molasses, and milk together. Add to the dry ingredients to form a soft dough.

6 On a lightly floured kitchen counter, roll out the dough to a thickness of ³/₄ inch and cut out 8 scones, using a 2-inch plain pastry cutter.

7 Arrange the scones on the prepared cookie sheet and bake in a preheated oven at 425°F for 8–10 minutes.

8 Transfer the scones to a wire rack and cool slightly before serving.

9 Serve split in half and spread with butter.

COOK'S TIP

These scones can be frozen, but are best defrosted and eaten within 1 month.

Cherry Scones

These are an alternative to traditional scones, using sweet candied cherries which not only create color, but add a distinct flavor.

Makes 8

INGREDIENTS

2 cups self-rising flour
1 tbsp superfine sugar
pinch of salt

$^1/_3$ cup butter, cut into small pieces
3 tbsp candied cherries, chopped

3 tbsp golden raisins
1 egg, beaten
$^1/_4$ cup milk

1 Lightly grease a cookie sheet with a little butter.

2 Sift together the flour, sugar, and salt into a mixing bowl and rub in the butter with your fingers until the scone mixture resembles breadcrumbs.

3 Stir in the candied cherries and golden raisins. Add the beaten egg.

4 Reserve 1 tablespoon of the milk for glazing, then add the remainder to the mixture. Mix together to form a soft dough.

5 On a lightly floured surface, roll out the dough to a thickness of $^3/_4$ inch and cut out 8 scones, using a 2-inch plain pastry cutter.

6 Place the scones on the cookie sheet and brush with the reserved milk.

7 Bake in a preheated oven at 425°F for 8–10 minutes, or until the scones are golden brown.

8 Let cool slightly on a wire rack, then serve split and buttered.

COOK'S TIP

These scones will freeze very successfully, but they are best defrosted and eaten within 1 month.

Cranberry Muffins

These savory muffins are an ideal accompaniment to soup, or they make a nice change from sweet cakes for serving with coffee.

Makes 18

INGREDIENTS

2 cups all-purpose flour
2 tsp baking powder
$^1/_2$ tsp salt

3 tbsp superfine sugar
4 tbsp butter, melted
2 eggs, beaten

$^3/_4$ cup milk
1 cup fresh cranberries
2 tbsp freshly grated Parmesan cheese

1 Lightly grease 2 muffin pans with a little butter

2 Sift the flour, baking powder, and salt into a mixing bowl. Stir in the superfine sugar until well combined.

3 In a separate bowl, mix the butter, beaten eggs, and milk together, then pour into the bowl of dry ingredients.

4 Mix lightly together until all of the ingredients are evenly combined, then stir in the fresh cranberries.

5 Divide the mixture between the prepared pans.

6 Sprinkle the grated Parmesan cheese over the top of each muffin mixture.

7 Bake in a preheated oven at 400°F for about 20 minutes, or until the cranberry muffins are well risen and a golden brown color.

8 Let the muffins cool slightly in the pans. Transfer the muffins to a wire rack and cool completely before serving.

VARIATION

For a sweet alternative to this recipe, replace the Parmesan cheese with raw crystal sugar in step 5, if you prefer.

Cookies

Nothing can compare with a homemade cookie for bringing a touch of pleasure to a coffee break or tea-time. This selection of delicious cookies and after-dinner treats will tantalize your taste buds and keep you coming back for more.

Tempting cookies like Citrus Crescents, Meringues, Chocolate Chip Cookies, and Gingernuts are quick, easy, and satisfying to make. You can easily vary the finished shape of Vanilla Hearts, Caraway Cookies, Lemon Jumbles, and Rosemary Cookies if you have a favorite cookie cutter! The possibilities for inventiveness when making cookies are endless.

For cookie making, you need the best ingredients: nuts should be as fresh as possible, use good quality dark and white chocolate, sugars should be unrefined pure cane sugars, and you will discover that the best cookies are made with butter.

Always cool cookies on a wire rack and then store them in an airtight container to keep them fresh.

Spiced Cookies

*These spicy cookies are perfect to serve with
fruit salad or ice cream for a very easy instant dessert.*

Makes about 24

INGREDIENTS

³/₄ cup sweet butter

1 cup dark muscovado sugar

2 cups all-purpose flour

pinch of salt

¹/₂ tsp baking soda

1 tsp ground cinnamon

¹/₂ tsp ground coriander

¹/₂ tsp ground nutmeg

¹/₄ tsp ground cloves

2 tbsp dark rum

1 Lightly grease 2 cookie sheets with a little butter.

2 Cream together the butter and sugar and beat until light and fluffy.

3 Sift the flour, salt, baking soda, cinnamon, coriander, nutmeg, and cloves into the creamed mixture and mix until well combined.

4 Stir the dark rum into the creamed mixture.

5 Using 2 teaspoons, place small mounds of the mixture onto the prepared cookie sheets 3 inches apart to allow for spreading during cooking. Flatten each mound slightly with the back of a spoon.

6 Bake in a preheated oven at 350°F for 10–12 minutes, until golden.

7 Let the cookies cool and crispen on wire racks before serving.

COOK'S TIP

*Use the back of a fork to flatten
the cookies slightly
before baking.*

Cinnamon & Sunflower Squares

These are moist cake-like squares with a lovely spicy flavor.

Makes 12

INGREDIENTS

1 cup butter, softened
1¼ cups superfine sugar
3 eggs, beaten

2 cups self-rising flour
½ tsp baking soda

1 tbsp ground cinnamon
⅔ cup sour cream
⅔ cup sunflower seeds

1 Grease a 9-inch square cake pan with a little butter and line the base with baking parchment.

2 Put the butter and superfine sugar into a large mixing bowl and cream them together until the mixture becomes light and fluffy.

3 Gradually add the beaten eggs to the mixture, beating well after each addition.

4 Sift the flour, baking soda, and ground cinnamon into

the creamed mixture and fold in gently, using a metal spoon.

5 Spoon in the sour cream and sunflower seeds and gently mix together until well combined.

6 Spoon the mixture into the prepared cake pan and level the surface with the back of a spoon or a knife.

7 Bake in a preheated oven at 350°F for about 45 minutes, or until the mixture is firm to the touch when pressed.

8 Loosen the edges with a round-bladed knife, then turn out onto a wire rack to cool completely. Slice into 12 squares.

COOK'S TIP

These moist squares will freeze well and keep for up to 1 month.

Gingernuts

*Nothing compares to the taste of these freshly baked authentic
gingernuts, which have a lovely hint of orange flavor.*

Makes 30

INGREDIENTS

3 cups self-rising flour
pinch of salt
1 cup superfine sugar

1 tbsp ground ginger
1 tsp baking soda
1/2 cup butter

1/4 cup light corn syrup
1 egg, beaten
1 tsp grated orange rind

1 Lightly grease several cookie sheets.

2 Sift the flour, salt, sugar, ginger, and baking soda into a large mixing bowl.

3 Heat the butter and light corn syrup together in a saucepan over a very low heat until the butter has completely melted.

4 Let the butter mixture cool slightly, then pour it onto the dry ingredients.

5 Add the egg and orange rind and mix thoroughly.

6 Using your hands, carefully shape the dough into 30 even-size balls.

7 Place the balls well apart on the prepared cookie sheets, then flatten them slightly with your fingers.

8 Bake in a preheated oven at 325°F for 15–20 minutes, then transfer them to a wire rack to cool before serving.

COOK'S TIP

*Store these cookies in an airtight
container and eat them
within 1 week.*

VARIATION

*If you like your gingernuts crunchy,
bake them in the oven for a
few minutes longer.*

Caraway Cookies

The caraway seed is best known for its appearance in old-fashioned seed cake.
Here, caraway seeds give these cookies a very distinctive flavor.

Makes about 36

INGREDIENTS

2 cups all-purpose flour
pinch of salt
1/3 cup butter, cut into small pieces

1¼ cups superfine sugar
1 egg, beaten

2 tbsp caraway seeds
raw crystal sugar, for sprinkling
(optional)

1 Lightly grease several cookie sheets.

2 Sift the flour and salt into a mixing bowl. Rub in the butter with your fingertips until the mixture resembles fine breadcrumbs. Stir in the superfine sugar.

3 Reserve 1 tablespoon of the beaten egg for brushing the cookies. Add the rest of the egg to the mixture, together with the caraway seeds and bring together to form a soft dough.

4 On a lightly floured surface, roll out the cookie dough thinly and then cut out about 36 rounds with a 2½-inch cookie cutter.

5 Transfer the cookies to the prepared cookie sheets, brush with the reserved beaten egg, and sprinkle with a little raw crystal sugar.

6 Bake in a preheated oven at 325°F for 10–15 minutes, until crisp and lightly golden in color.

7 Let the cookies cool on a wire rack and store in an airtight container.

VARIATION

Caraway seeds have a nutty, delicate anise flavor. If you don't like their flavor, replace the caraway seeds with the milder-flavored poppy seeds.

Peanut Butter Cookies

*These crunchy cookies will be popular with children
of all ages as they contain their favorite food—peanut butter.*

Makes 20

INGREDIENTS

¹/₂ cup butter, softened
¹/₂ cup chunky peanut butter
1 cup sugar

1 egg, lightly beaten
1¹/₄ cups all-purpose flour
¹/₂ tsp baking powder

pinch of salt
³/₄ cup unsalted natural peanuts,
   chopped

1 Lightly grease 2 cookie sheets.

2 In a large mixing bowl, beat together the butter and peanut butter.

3 Gradually add the sugar and beat well.

4 Add the beaten egg, a little at a time, beating until it is thoroughly combined.

5 Sift the flour, baking powder, and salt into the peanut butter mixture.

6 Add the peanuts and bring all of the ingredients together to form a soft dough. Wrap and chill for about 30 minutes.

7 Form the dough into 20 balls and place them onto the prepared cookie sheets about 2 inches apart to allow for spreading. Flatten them slightly with a fork.

8 Bake in a preheated oven at 375°F for 15 minutes, until a golden brown color. Transfer the cookies to a wire rack and cool slightly.

COOK'S TIP

For a crunchy bite and sparkling appearance, sprinkle the cookies with raw crystal sugar before baking.

Hazelnut Squares

These can be made quickly and easily for an afternoon treat.
The chopped hazelnuts can be replaced by any other nut of your choice.

Makes 16

INGREDIENTS

1¹/₄ cups all-purpose flour
pinch of salt
1 tsp baking powder

¹/₃ cup butter, cut into small pieces
1 cup light brown sugar
1 egg, beaten
4 tbsp milk

1 cup hazelnuts, halved
raw crystal sugar, for sprinkling
(optional)

1 Grease a 9-inch square cake pan and line the base with baking parchment.

2 Sift the flour, salt, and baking powder into a large mixing bowl.

3 Rub in the butter with your fingers until the mixture resembles fine breadcrumbs. Stir in the brown sugar.

4 Add the egg, milk, and nuts to the mixture and stir well until thoroughly combined.

5 Spoon the mixture into the prepared cake pan and level the surface. Sprinkle with raw crystal sugar, if using.

6 Bake in a preheated oven at 350°F for about 25 minutes, or until the mixture is firm to the touch when pressed with a finger.

7 Cool slightly for 10 minutes, then loosen the edges with a round-bladed knife, and turn out onto a wire rack to cool further. Cut into squares.

VARIATION

For a coffee time cookie, replace the milk with the same amount of cold strong black coffee—the stronger the better!

Coconut Cookies

Freshly baked, these chewy cookies make a great snack.

Makes 16 squares

INGREDIENTS

1 cup butter
1^1/$_3$ cups raw crystal sugar

2 tbsp light corn syrup
3^1/$_2$ cups dried oats
1 cup shredded coconut

^{1}/$_3$ cup candied cherries, chopped

1 Lightly grease a 12 x 9-inch cookie sheet.

2 Heat the butter, raw crystal sugar, and light corn syrup in a large saucepan over a low heat until just melted.

3 Stir in the oats, shredded coconut, and candied cherries and mix well until evenly combined.

4 Spread the mixture onto the cookie sheet and press down with the back of a spatula to make a smooth surface.

5 Bake in a preheated oven at 325°F for about 30 minutes.

6 Remove from the oven and cool on the cookie sheet for 10 minutes.

7 Cut the mixture into squares using a sharp knife.

8 Carefully transfer the squares to a wire rack and cool completely.

COOK'S TIP

These cookies are best stored in an airtight container and eaten within 1 week. They can also be frozen for up to 1 month.

Oat & Raisin Cookies

These oaty, fruity cookies are delicious with a cup of tea!

Makes 10

INGREDIENTS

4 tbsp butter
$^1/_2$ cup superfine sugar
1 egg, beaten

$^1/_2$ cup all-purpose flour
$^1/_2$ tsp salt
$^1/_2$ tsp baking powder

2 cups oats
$^3/_4$ cup raisins
2 tbsp sesame seeds

1 Lightly grease 2 cookie sheets.

2 In a large mixing bowl, cream together the butter and sugar until light and fluffy.

3 Add the beaten egg gradually and beat until well combined.

4 Sift the flour, salt and baking powder into the creamed mixture. Mix well.

5 Add the oats, raisins, and sesame seeds and mix together thoroughly.

6 Place spoonfuls of the mixture well apart (to allow for spreading during baking) on the prepared cookie sheets and flatten them slightly with the back of a spoon.

7 Bake the cookies in a preheated oven at 350°F for 15 minutes.

8 Let the cookies cool slightly on the cookie sheets.

9 Transfer the cookies to a wire rack and cool completely before serving.

VARIATION

Substitute chopped ready-to-eat dried apricots for the raisins, if you prefer.

COOK'S TIP

To enjoy these cookies at their best, store them in an airtight container.

Rosemary Cookies

Do not be put off by the idea of herbs being used in these crisp cookies—try them and you will be pleasantly surprised.

Makes about 25

INGREDIENTS

2 tbsp butter, softened
4 tbsp superfine sugar
grated rind of 1 lemon
4 tbsp lemon juice

1 egg, separated
2 tsp finely chopped fresh rosemary
1 3/4 cups all-purpose flour, sifted

superfine sugar, for sprinkling (optional)

1 Lightly grease 2 cookie sheets.

2 In a large mixing bowl, cream together the butter and sugar until pale and fluffy.

3 Add the lemon rind and juice, then the egg yolk, and beat until they are thoroughly combined. Stir in the chopped fresh rosemary.

4 Add the sifted flour, mixing well until a soft dough is formed. Wrap and chill for 30 minutes.

5 On a lightly floured surface, roll out the dough thinly and stamp out about 25 cookies with a 2½-inch cookie cutter. Arrange the dough on the prepared cookie sheets.

6 In a small bowl, lightly beat the egg white. Gently brush the egg white over the surface of each cookie, then sprinkle with a little superfine sugar, if desired.

7 Bake the cookies in a preheated oven at 350°F for about 15 minutes.

8 Transfer the cookies to a wire rack and cool completely before serving.

COOK'S TIP

Store the cookies in an airtight container for up to 1 week.

VARIATION

In place of the fresh rosemary, use 1½ teaspoons of dried rosemary, if you prefer.

Citrus Crescents

*For a sweet treat, try these cookies which
have a lovely citrus tang to them.*

Makes about 25

INGREDIENTS

$^1/_3$ cup butter, softened
$^1/_3$ cup superfine sugar
1 egg, separated

$1^3/_4$ cups all-purpose flour
grated rind of 1 orange
grated rind of 1 lemon

grated rind of 1 lime
2–3 tbsp orange juice
superfine sugar, for sprinkling
(optional)

1 Lightly grease 2 cookie sheets.

2 In a mixing bowl, cream together the butter and sugar until light and fluffy, then gradually beat in the egg yolk.

3 Sift the flour into the creamed mixture and mix until evenly combined. Add the orange, lemon, and lime rinds to the mixture with enough of the orange juice to make a soft dough.

4 Roll out the dough on a lightly floured surface. Stamp out cookies using a 3-inch cookie cutter. Make crescent shapes by cutting away a quarter of each cookie. Re-roll the pastry trimmings to make about 25 crescents.

5 Prick the surface of each crescent with a fork. Place the crescents onto the prepared cookie sheets.

6 Lightly beat the egg white in a small bowl and gently brush it over the cookies. Dust the cookies with extra superfine sugar, if using.

7 Bake in a preheated oven at 400°F for 12–15 minutes. Transfer the cookies to a wire rack and cool slightly before serving.

COOK'S TIP

*Store the citrus crescents in an
airtight container. Alternatively,
they can be frozen for up
to 1 month.*

Lemon Jumbles

*These lemony, melt-in-your-mouth cookies are made extra special
by dredging with confectioners' sugar just before serving.*

Makes about 50

INGREDIENTS

¹/₃ cup butter, softened	1 egg, beaten	1 tsp baking powder
¹/₂ cup superfine sugar	4 tbsp lemon juice	1 tbsp milk
grated rind of 1 lemon	3 cups all-purpose flour	confectioners' sugar, for dredging

1 Lightly grease several cookie sheets.

2 In a mixing bowl, cream together the butter, superfine sugar, and lemon rind until pale and fluffy.

3 Add the beaten egg and lemon juice a little at a time, beating well after each addition.

4 Sift the flour and baking powder into the creamed mixture and blend together until well combined. Add the milk, mixing to form a dough.

5 Turn the dough out onto a lightly floured working surface and divide into about 50 equal-size pieces.

6 Roll each piece into a sausage shape with your hands and twist in the middle to make an "S" shape.

7 Place the shapes on the prepared cookie sheets and bake in a preheated oven at 325°F for 15–20 minutes. Cool completely on a wire rack before serving. Dredge with confectioners' sugar to serve.

VARIATION

If you prefer, shape the dough into other shapes—letters of the alphabet or geometric shapes—or just make into round cookies.

Chocolate & Lemon Pinwheels

These stunning cookies will have your guests guessing what mystery ingredients give the pinwheels their exotic flavor!

Makes about 40

INGREDIENTS

$^3/_4$ cup butter, softened
$1^1/_3$ cups superfine sugar

1 egg, beaten
3 cups all-purpose flour

1 ounce dark chocolate, melted and cooled slightly
grated rind of 1 lemon

1 Grease and flour several cookie sheets.

2 In a large mixing bowl, cream together the butter and sugar until light and fluffy.

3 Gradually add the beaten egg to the creamed mixture, beating well after each addition.

4 Sift the flour into the creamed mixture and mix until a soft dough forms.

5 Transfer half of the dough to another bowl and beat in the cooled melted chocolate.

6 Stir the grated lemon rind into the other half of the plain dough.

7 On a lightly floured surface, roll out the 2 pieces of dough to form rectangles of the same size.

8 Lay the lemon dough on top of the chocolate dough. Roll up the dough tightly into a sausage shape, using a sheet of baking parchment to guide you. Let the dough chill slightly in the refrigerator.

9 Cut the roll into about 40 slices, place them on the

cookie sheets, and bake in a preheated oven at 375°F for 10–12 minutes, or until lightly golden. Transfer the pinwheels to a wire rack and cool completely before serving.

COOK'S TIP

To make rolling out easier, place each piece of dough between 2 sheets of baking parchment.

White Chocolate Cookies

These chunky cookies melt in your mouth and the white chocolate gives them a deliciously rich flavor.

Makes 24

INGREDIENTS

$^1/_2$ cup butter, softened
$^3/_4$ cup light brown sugar
1 egg, beaten

$1^3/_4$ cups self-rising flour
pinch of salt

$4^1/_2$ ounces white chocolate,
   roughly chopped
$^1/_2$ cup chopped Brazil nuts

1 Lightly grease several cookie sheets.

2 In a large mixing bowl, cream together the butter and sugar until light and fluffy.

3 Gradually add the beaten egg to the creamed mixture, beating well after each addition.

4 Sift the flour and salt into the creamed mixture and blend well.

5 Stir in the white chocolate chunks and Brazil nuts.

6 Place heaping teaspoons of the white chocolate mixture onto the prepared cookie sheets. Do not put more than 6 teaspoons of the mixture onto each cookie sheet as the cookies will spread considerably during cooking.

7 Bake in a preheated oven at 375°F for 10–12 minutes, or until the cookies are a light golden brown color.

8 Transfer the cookies to wire racks and set aside until completely cold and crisp before serving.

VARIATION

Use dark or milk chocolate instead of white chocolate, if you prefer.

Shortbread Fantails

*These cookies are perfect with tea or they can
be served with ice cream for a delicious dessert.*

Makes 8

INGREDIENTS

$^1/_2$ cup butter, softened
$^1/_4$ cup sugar
$^1/_4$ cup confectioners' sugar
2 cups all-purpose flour

pinch of salt
2 tsp orange flower water
superfine sugar, for sprinkling

1 Lightly grease an 8-inch
shallow round cake pan with
a little butter.

2 In a large mixing bowl, cream
together the butter, the sugar,
and the confectioners' sugar until
light and fluffy.

3 Sift the flour and salt into the
creamed mixture. Add the
orange flower water and bring
everything together to form a
soft dough.

4 On a lightly floured surface,
roll out the dough to an
8-inch round and place in the pan.

Prick the dough well and score
into 8 triangles with a round-
bladed knife.

5 Bake in a preheated oven at
300°F for 30–35 minutes, or
until the cookie is crisp and pale
golden in color.

6 Sprinkle with a little
superfine sugar, then cut
along the marked lines to make
the fantails.

7 Let the shortbread cool
completely before removing
the pieces from the pan. Store in
an airtight container.

COOK'S TIP

*For a crunchy addition, sprinkle
2 tablespoons of chopped mixed
nuts over the top of the fantails
before baking.*

Millionaire's Shortbread

These rich squares of shortbread are topped with caramel and finished with chocolate to make a very special treat!

Makes 12 bars

INGREDIENTS

1¹/₂ cups all-purpose flour
¹/₂ cup butter, cut into small pieces

3 tbsp light brown sugar, sifted

TOPPING:
4 tbsp butter
3 tbsp light brown sugar

14 ounce can condensed milk
5¹/₂ ounces milk chocolate

1 Thoroughly grease a 9-inch square cake pan.

2 Sift the flour into a mixing bowl and rub in the butter with your fingertips until the mixture resembles fine breadcrumbs. Add the sugar and mix to form a firm dough.

3 Press the dough into the bottom of the prepared pan and prick with a fork.

4 Bake in a preheated oven at 375°F for 20 minutes, until lightly golden. Cool completely in the pan.

5 To make the topping, place the butter, sugar, and condensed milk in a nonstick saucepan and cook over a gentle heat, stirring constantly, until the mixture comes to a boil.

6 Reduce the heat and cook for 4–5 minutes, until the caramel is pale golden and thick and is coming away from the sides of the pan. Pour over the shortbread base and let cool.

7 When the caramel topping is firm, melt the milk chocolate in a double boiler. Spread the melted chocolate over the topping, set aside in a cool place, then cut the shortbread into squares or bars to serve.

COOK'S TIP

Ensure the caramel layer is completely cool and set before coating it with the melted chocolate, otherwise they will mix together.

Vanilla Hearts

This is a classic shortbread cookie which melts in your mouth. Here the cookies are made in pretty heart shapes which will appeal to everyone.

Makes about 16

INGREDIENTS

2 cups all-purpose flour
$^2/_3$ cup butter, cut into small pieces

$^1/_2$ cup superfine sugar
1 tsp vanilla extract

superfine sugar, for dusting

1 Lightly grease a cookie sheet with a little butter.

2 Sift the flour into a large mixing bowl and rub in the butter with your fingers until the mixture is well combined and resembles fine breadcrumbs.

3 Stir in the superfine sugar and vanilla extract and bring the mixture together with your hands to make a firm dough.

4 On a lightly floured surface, roll out the dough to a thickness of about 1 inch. Stamp out 12 heart shapes with a heart-shaped cookie cutter measuring about 2 inches across and 1 inch deep.

5 Arrange the hearts on the prepared cookie sheet. Bake in a preheated oven at 350°F for 15–20 minutes, until the hearts are a light golden color.

6 Transfer the vanilla hearts to a wire rack and cool slightly. Dust with a little superfine sugar, if desired, just before serving.

COOK'S TIP

Place a fresh vanilla bean in your superfine sugar and keep it in a storage jar for several weeks to give the sugar a delicious vanilla flavor.

Rock Drops

These rock drops are more substantial than a crisp cookie.
Serve them fresh from the oven to enjoy them at their best.

Makes 8

INGREDIENTS

1³/4 cups all-purpose flour
2 tsp baking powder
1/3 cup butter, cut into small pieces

1/3 cup raw crystal sugar
1/2 cup golden raisins

2 tbsp candied cherries,
    finely chopped
1 egg, beaten
2 tbsp milk

1 Lightly grease a cookie sheet.

2 Sift the flour and baking powder into a mixing bowl. Rub in the butter with your fingers until the mixture resembles breadcrumbs.

3 Stir in the raw crystal sugar, golden raisins, and chopped candied cherries.

4 Add the beaten egg and the milk to the mixture and mix to form a soft dough.

5 Spoon 8 mounds of the mixture onto the cookie sheet, spacing them well apart as they will spread while they are cooking.

6 Bake in a preheated oven at 400°F for 15–20 minutes, until firm to the touch when pressed with a finger.

7 Remove the rock drops from the cookie sheet. Either serve piping hot from the oven or transfer to a wire rack and let cool before serving.

COOK'S TIP

For convenience, prepare the dry ingredients in advance and just before cooking stir in the liquid.

Chocolate Chip Brownies

Choose a good quality chocolate for these chocolate chip brownies to give them a rich flavor that is not too sweet.

Makes 12

INGREDIENTS

5¹/2 ounces dark chocolate, broken into pieces
1 cup butter, softened
2 cups self-rising flour

¹/2 cup superfine sugar
4 eggs, beaten
³/4 cup chopped pistachio nuts

3¹/2 ounces white chocolate, roughly chopped
confectioners' sugar, for dusting

1 Lightly grease a 9-inch baking pan and line with wax paper.

2 Melt the dark chocolate and butter in a double boiler. Leave to cool slightly.

3 Sift the flour into a separate mixing bowl and stir in the superfine sugar.

4 Stir the eggs into the melted chocolate mixture, then pour this mixture into the flour and sugar mixture, beating well. Stir in the pistachio nuts and white

chocolate, then pour the mixture into the pan, spreading it evenly into the corners.

5 Bake in a preheated oven at 350° for 30–35 minutes, until firm to the touch. Cool in the pan for about 20 minutes, then turn out onto a wire rack to cool further.

6 Dust the surface of the cookies with a little confectioners' sugar and cut into 12 pieces when completely cold and crisp.

COOK'S TIP

The brownie won't be completely firm in the middle when it is removed from the oven, but it will set when it has cooled.

Chocolate Biscotti

These dry cookies are delicious served
with black coffee after a meal.

Makes 16

INGREDIENTS

1 egg
1¹/₃ cup superfine sugar
1 tsp vanilla extract

1 cup all-purpose flour
¹/₂ tsp baking powder
1 tsp ground cinnamon

1³/₄ ounces dark chocolate,
  roughly chopped
¹/₂ cup toasted slivered almonds
¹/₂ cup pine nuts

1 Grease a large cookie sheet with a little butter

2 Beat the egg, sugar, and vanilla extract in a mixing bowl with an electric mixer until it is thick and pale—ribbons of mixture should trail from the beater as you lift it.

3 Sift the flour, baking powder, and cinnamon into a separate bowl, then sift into the egg mixture and fold in gently. Stir in the chocolate, slivered almonds, and pine nuts.

4 Turn out onto a lightly floured surface and shape into a flat log about 9 inches long and ¾ inch wide. Transfer to the prepared cookie sheet.

5 Bake in a preheated oven at 350°F for 20–25 minutes, or until golden. Remove from the oven and cool for 5 minutes, or until firm.

6 Transfer the log to a cutting board. Using a serrated bread knife, cut the log on the diagonal into slices about ½ inch thick and

arrange them on the cookie sheet. Cook for 10–15 minutes, turning halfway through the cooking time.

7 Cool for about 5 minutes, then transfer to a wire rack to cool completely.

COOK'S TIP

Store the biscotti in an
airtight container or jar and eat
within 2 weeks.

Chocolate Macaroons

*Classic sticky macaroons are always a favorite: they
are made even better by the addition of rich dark chocolate.*

Makes 18

INGREDIENTS

2 ³/₄ ounces dark chocolate, broken
    into pieces
2 egg whites

pinch of salt
1 cup superfine sugar

1 ¹/₄ cups ground almonds
shredded coconut, for sprinkling
    (optional)

1 Grease 2 cookie sheets with
a little butter and line
with baking parchment or
rice paper.

2 Melt the dark chocolate in a
double boiler, then cool
slightly.

3 In a mixing bowl, beat the
egg whites with the salt until
they form soft peaks.

4 Gradually whisk the
superfine sugar into the egg
whites, then fold in the almonds
and cooled melted chocolate.

5 Place heaping teaspoonfuls
of the mixture spaced well
apart on the prepared cookie sheets
and spread into drops about
2½ inches across. Sprinkle
with a little shredded coconut,
if desired.

6 Bake in a preheated oven at
300°F for about 25 minutes,
or until firm.

7 Cool slightly before carefully
lifting the chocolate
macaroons from the cookie sheets.
Transfer to a wire rack and cool
completely before serving.

COOK'S TIP

*Store the macaroons in an airtight
container and eat within 1 week.*

VARIATION

*For a traditional
finish, top each
macaroon with half
a candied cherry before
baking them.*

Florentines

*These luxury cookies will be popular at any time
of the year but make a wonderful treat for Christmastime.*

Makes 8–10

INGREDIENTS

4 tbsp butter
$1/4$ cup superfine sugar
$2^1/4$ cup all-purpose flour, sifted

$1/3$ cup almonds, chopped
$1/3$ cup chopped candied peel
$1/4$ cup raisins, chopped

2 tbsp candied cherries, chopped
finely grated rind of $1/2$ lemon
$4^1/2$ ounces dark chocolate, melted

1 Line 2 large cookie sheets with baking parchment.

2 Heat the butter and superfine sugar in a small saucepan until the butter has just melted and the sugar dissolved. Remove the pan from the heat.

3 Stir in the flour and mix until well combined. Stir in the chopped almonds, candied peel, raisins, cherries and lemon rind and mix together well. Place teaspoonfuls of the mixture well apart on the cookie sheets.

4 Bake in a preheated oven at 350°F for 10 minutes, or until lightly golden in color.

5 As soon as the florentines are removed from the oven, press the edges into neat shapes while still on the cookie sheets, using a cookie cutter. Cool on the cookie sheets until firm, then carefully transfer to a wire rack to cool completely.

6 Spread the melted chocolate over the smooth side of each florentine. As the chocolate begins to set, mark wavy lines or the pattern of your choice in it with a fork. Leave the florentines until set, chocolate side up.

VARIATION

Replace the dark chocolate with white chocolate or, for a dramatic effect, cover half of the florentines in dark chocolate and half in white.

Meringues

These are just as meringues should be—as light as air and at the same time crisp and melt in your mouth.

Makes about 13

INGREDIENTS

4 egg whites
pinch of salt
1/2 cup sugar

1/2 cup superfine sugar
1 1/4 cups heavy cream,
    whipped lightly

1 Line 3 cookie sheets with a few sheets of baking parchment.

2 In a large clean bowl, whisk together the egg whites and salt until they are stiff, using an electric mixer. (You should be able to turn the bowl upside down without any movement from the egg whites.)

3 Carefully beat the sugar into the egg white mixture a little at a time; the meringue should start to look glossy at this stage.

4 Sprinkle in the superfine sugar, a little at a time, and continue beating until all the sugar has been incorporated and the meringue is thick, white, and stands in tall peaks.

5 Transfer the meringue mixture to a pastry bag fitted with a 3/4-inch star tip. Pipe about 26 small whirls onto the prepared cookie sheets.

6 Bake in a preheated oven at 250°F for 1½ hours, or until the meringues are pale golden in color and can be easily lifted off

the paper. Cool in the turned-off oven overnight.

7 Just before serving, sandwich the meringues together in pairs with the cream and arrange on a serving plate.

VARIATION

For a finer texture, replace the ordinary sugar with superfine sugar.